Saskatchewan
HEROES
& ROGUES

Saskatchewan HEROES & ROGUES

Ruth Wright Millar

© Ruth Wright Millar, 2004

All rights reserved. No part of this publication may be reproduced, stored in a retrieval system or transmitted, in any form or by any means, without the prior written consent of the publisher or a licence from The Canadian Copyright Licensing Agency (Access Copyright). For an Access Copyright licence, visit www.accesscopyright.ca or call toll free to 1-800-893-5777.

Edited by Roberta Mitchell Coulter
Book and cover design by Duncan Campbell
Printed and bound in Canada at Gauvin Press

National Library of Canada Cataloguing in Publication Data

Millar, Ruth
Saskatchewan heroes & rogues / Ruth Wright Millar.

Includes bibliographical references.
ISBN 1-55050-289-1

1. Saskatchewan—Biography. I. Title. II. Title: Saskatchewan heroes and rogues.

FC3505.M54 2004   971.24'009'9   C2004-901626-1

POD June 2012

2517 Victoria Avenue
Regina, Saskatchewan
Canada   S4P 0T2
www.coteaubooks.com

Available in Canada from:
Publishers Group Canada
2440 Viking Way
Richmond, British Columbia
Canada   V6V 1N2

Coteau Books gratefully acknowledges the financial support of its publishing program by: the Saskatchewan Arts Board, the Canada Council for the Arts, the Government of Canada through the Canada Book Fund, the Government of Saskatchewan through the Creative Economy Entrepreneurial Fund and the City of Regina Arts Commission.

*To my family and friends
who were so generous
in their support and encouragement of me
in this obsession of mine.*

Contents

Introduction – i

Kathleen Rice – 1
Ernest Dufault, alias Will James – 15
Charlie Parmer – 29
Big Tom Hourie – 39
Norman Falkner – 57
Morris "Two-Gun" Cohen – 67
Jean Ewen – 87
Gladys Arnold – 107
Father John Claffey – 121
Joan Bamford Fletcher – 133
Emma Woikin – 147
Richard St. Barbe Baker – 163

Endnotes – 179
Acknowledgments – 199

Introduction

History is somewhat capricious in whom and what it chooses to remember. In Saskatchewan we have a galaxy of well-celebrated personalities – politicians like Louis Riel, Gabriel Dumont, Tommy Douglas, and John Diefenbaker; athletes like Ethel Catherwood, George Genereux, Diane Jones-Konihowski, Catriona LeMay Doan, and Gordie Howe; and well-known performers including Joni Mitchell, Buffy Sainte-Marie, and Murray Adaskin. This book is not about them. Nor is it about other politicians, entrepreneurs, or sports heroes whose lives have already been well-documented.

Saskatchewan Heroes and Rogues is intended to rescue from oblivion some lesser-known heroes, rascals, adventurers, and trailblazers in our colourful past and thrust them back into the limelight. This book also attempts to prevent other, older and forgotten books about these characters from being thrown in the trash bin.

The quality that links these extraordinary people is *audacity*. Most of them had a profound belief in themselves or their own convictions, or were driven by an unquenchable will to survive. Some achieved a degree of national or international fame, but their Saskatchewan connection is little known. Others are simply obscure, though their exploits are recorded in books that now languish in library storage. Most enjoyed their brief hour upon the stage, their life stories recorded in a rush of articles, and then were heard of no more. Their names may stir flashes of memory amongst old-timers, but young people have never heard of them.

Not all these people were heroic – some were downright rascals – but we love our scallywags as well as our heroes. And while the transgressions of pickpockets and bank robbers could be presented with a wink and a nod, I drew the line at the truly evil ones – the Nazis and the Ku Klux Klan, for example, who were active in the province at one time. The scale of their wickedness seemed to be of a different dimension.

Few of these lives were blighted by missed opportunities or roads not taken. Most were doers and achieved their goals. Once a decision was made or a turning point passed, they usually drew on their own resources of talent, intelligence, courage, or perseverance to triumph over adversity.

The stories told here represent certain themes, reflecting my own fascination with physical courage, social activism, espionage, and heroism in war. Others were buffeted by chance in their personal circumstances or by broad human tides such as economic depression or war. They were in a certain time and place at a fateful moment, or they happened to know someone who nudged them into a fateful act or choice. Father Claffey, for example, was living in the Vatican when fugitives began flowing to Rome in war-torn Italy, and he joined a clandestine escape organization to shelter them from the Nazis. Emma Woikin would probably have stayed in Blaine Lake if not for personal calamity and poverty that drew her into political intrigue in Ottawa. There, chance nudged her into a job as a cipher clerk in the Dept. of External Affairs, where the Russians exploited her extraordinary memory. Journalist Gladys Arnold's presence in France just as that country fell to the Nazis defined the rest of her life.

There were multiple twists and turns in their lives. Norman Falkner's life was profoundly altered by the loss of a leg in wartime, but he overcame his handicap in a flamboyant way. Crippling injuries also forced Will James to abandon bronco-busting for writing and drawing. Two-Gun Cohen blundered into an attempted robbery, defended a Chinese man, and was ushered into their exotic world.

But in almost all cases, they took decisive steps in pursuit of their own goals. Arnold *decided* to go to France in the thirties. Kate Rice *decided* to leave Ontario, first for Saskatchewan and then the northern bush. Will

James left his family at the age of fifteen and headed west to become a cowboy. Charlie Parmer supposedly renounced a rip-roaring outlaw life in the United States to live in relative peace and security in Dundurn.

Jean Ewen's response to the misery of the Depression was to accept a better-paying but hazardous nursing job in China, long before Dr. Bethune went there. Then she risked her life to save the lives of injured Chinese during the Japanese bombardment. Richard St. Barbe Baker chose trees as his life's cause, becoming an environmental activist and a harbinger of the entire movement.

Several of these people were masters of deception, illusion, or outright fakery. Parmer actually had worked as a circus faker. Woikin moved in the shadowy world of espionage after World War II. Like Grey Owl (who is not included in this book because his story is already so well documented), Will James adopted a new identity in one of the most remarkable deceptions in North American literature.

Other writers have written about rogues, rascals, and outright criminals among us since early days, so only a few were included in this volume. In their declining years, these rascals often undertook a quest for redemption. Alleged bank robber Parmer may have ridden with the Jesse James gang, but the latter part of his life suggested flight from an outlaw past, an attempt to go straight. Still, he slept with a gun under his pillow, fearing his shadowy past might catch up with him. Two-Gun Cohen was a pickpocket and ne'er-do-well in Saskatoon, but later redeemed himself somewhat as bodyguard to Sun Yat-sen and an honorary general in the Chinese Nationalist Army.

Will James may or may not have been involved in a barroom shoot-out, but his foray into the world of cattle rustling and subsequent imprisonment is a matter of record. He rose above all this by becoming one of the most renowned and beloved cowboy artists and storytellers of the American West. Whatever her motives, Emma Woikin chose to aid the Russians in supposed espionage activities during the war, was jailed in the Kingston pen, but ended up a respectable matron, working as a crack secretary in some of Saskatoon's most prestigious law firms.

Trailblazing and courage are other prominent themes in these lives. The trailblazers pushed into new frontiers, physically or occupationally.

Kathleen Rice braved the northern wilds, in search of precious metals and furs, defying public opinion as to a woman's proper role. Arnold brazenly ventured into Nazi territory and later fled from France while fighter planes zoomed over her head. Tom Hourie supposedly swam across the treacherous, icy waters of the South Saskatchewan River in March during the Northwest Resistance, and galloped through a blizzard of bullets in combat. Will James battled fearsome wild horses. Joan Bamford Fletcher shepherded civilian internees out of a Japanese prison camp through a rebel-infested jungle to safety. My personal favourite is the story of Jean Ewen's trek across war-torn China with Dr. Norman Bethune, and her miraculous escapes from death under continuing aerial bombardment. All these people in their own way showed stamina and grit.

Such tales prove that courage has no gender. These women also chose daring and unusual paths. Until recent decades, most women were much more restricted by their role as wives and mothers, as day care and shared parenting weren't the norm. It isn't just coincidence that some of the adventurous women in this book ignored the biological imperative, forgoing marriage and children, as did early trapper and miner Rice, and war hero Fletcher. Thus they escaped the usual barriers to career achievement for women.

All these people to some extent defied the conventions of their day. Some could legitimately be called eccentrics. The spotlight on their pasts helps to explain their eccentricities, as in the cases of Parmer, Rice, and Baker.

Many of the biographies are tinged with sorrow, even tragedy. Some were alcoholics, driven to extremes by stress and disappointments in their lives. Others were womanizers or were so restless they couldn't stay put, and their marriages fell apart. These were all real people, if flawed.

All these people deserve recognition and should be household names in this province and across the country. Their stories are meant to whet the reader's appetite for more such tales, and perhaps stimulate the writing of full-length biographies where such are lacking. There are legions of other extraordinary but little-known figures in Saskatchewan history.

Kathleen Rice at Herb/Wekusko Lake, 1914. – *Courtesy of St. Marys Museum, Ontario.*

KATHLEEN RICE
Gun-toting Prospector

Early in the twentieth century, a stunningly beautiful woman roamed alone through the northern wilds, hunting, trapping, and prospecting. In winter she mushed by dogsled over frozen lakes and trails. In summer she paddled her canoe through whitewater rapids. She shot wolves and fended off bears. Brandishing a shotgun, she shooed away suspected claim jumpers, and sent amorous miners packing – except perhaps for one. But news stories of her lucky strike did not unearth the secret she hid from most of the world.

Kathleen Creighton Starr Rice was no brawny Brunhilda. As a young woman she was pale and ethereal-looking, with searing blue-green eyes and masses of blonde hair piled atop her head. She was tall and willowy, and if she were young today, she could be sauntering along the fashion runways of Paris or Milan. Some photos reflect her intensity and steely will. Her voice was "low-pitched, contralto in tone."[1] On visits to Toronto she wore ladylike clothes, sometimes out of date after her long absences. She was clever and university-educated, specializing in natural sciences and mathematics. Publishers accepted her manuscripts. But she ignored all these genteel gifts and went off in search of adventure on the northern frontier.

During the first world war, after she had adopted the north, Rice bobbed her long hair, long before twenties-era flappers did so. She traded her bothersome long skirts for trappers' and miners' gear, wearing moccasins or miners' hobnailed boots and men's breeches. On a trip to her Ontario home town she strode through the streets in a long black coat and a bearskin hat. Despite these mannish get-ups, in the isolation of the northern woods she must have been a heavenly sight to lonely prospectors, but she fended them off with an acid tongue.

Kathleen Rice was born in 1883 and grew up in St. Marys in southwestern Ontario. One branch of her distinguished family had Irish roots. Other ancestors had been Pilgrims, and there was a rumoured family connection with Abraham Lincoln.

Kathleen was the image of her tall, fair-haired father, Henry Lincoln Rice. A graduate of Victoria College, majoring in classics, he taught at Dr. Tassie's School, a respected collegiate in Galt, Ontario. Her grandfather was the Reverend Dr. Samuel Dwight Rice, born in Maine in 1815. A convert to Methodism, he founded a college for women in Hamilton (a fairly radical idea in its day). Her mother was Lottie Carter, the daughter of wealthy St. Marys businessman George Carter, who had emigrated from County Tipperary in Ireland and forged a prosperous wheat brokerage.

According to Kathleen's biographer, Lottie was unambitious, unremarkable, and bound by social conventions. Kathleen preferred her father, who taught her to hunt and shoot. Although he himself had abandoned dreams of frontier adventure for a serene, conventional life, he infected his daughter with an intrepid vagabond spirit. Perhaps she committed herself to living out his fantasy of roaming the woods like Daniel Boone.

At the University of Toronto, Rice's pet subjects were mathematics, astronomy, and physics – unusual for a female student – and she won the Edward Blake scholarship.[2] Her literary flair must have surfaced by then, for she was active in the Women's Literary Society. Already keen on women's issues, she was secretary of the YWCA. Rice graduated in 1906 with an honours degree in mathematics.

She veered close to living out a traditional life as wife and mother when a young divinity student supposedly proposed to her, but he died unexpectedly. The semi-fictional account of her life has her admirer, Ken, die suddenly on the tennis court.

Freed from the prospect of marriage, Rice became a teacher, one of the few jobs available to women of her time. She received her Ontario high school teaching certificate in 1909, and another in Saskatchewan in 1912.[3] Mathematics was her specialty, so she taught that. She was a teacher in several Ontario schools, then came west and taught at Keys, Alberta, and finally at Yorkton, Saskatchewan, where she taught from January to July, 1912.[4] Peeved at the eyebrows raised over a woman teaching mathematics, Rice dropped the teaching profession. She fled to the wilderness of the Rockies,

Kathleen Rice, ca. 1906. – *Courtesy St. Marys Museum, Ontario*

learned to ski, and joined the Alpine Ski Club. As she stood alone on those remote mountain slopes she realized that the wilderness was her natural habitat.

Homesteading appealed to her, but it was impossible for a single woman who was not the head of a family to get a homestead.[5] She wheedled her brother, George Dwight Lincoln Rice, into coming out west in 1913 and applying for homestead land near The Pas in 1913, where the rail line ended.[6] The application was in his name, but she worked at clearing the quarter section. Lincoln returned to Ontario in the fall to pursue studies at the University of Toronto.

Left alone, Rice soon began to tire of the bucolic, rooted life of a farmer. Her gaze shifted toward the mineral-rich vastness beyond The Pas. Ever since the gold rushes in California, the Cariboo, and the Klondike, many adventurous spirits on prairie farms were seized by the lust for instant riches. In 1913 or perhaps earlier, gold had been found at Beaver (now Amisk) Lake, triggering a mini-gold rush to the area.[7] Farmers and other mining greenhorns known as cheechakos poured into

Fischer Avenue, main street of The Pas, ca. 1920s. *Courtesy of the Sam Waller Museum, The Pas.*

The Pas hoping to strike it rich. (Some, she remembered years later, were so naïve they planted their stakes in snow over the frozen lakes.) It was easy enough to travel by boat from Cumberland House, Saskatchewan, to The Pas, but newly arrived prospectors heading north by canoe to Beaver Lake first had to get to Namew Lake. From there, the route north was upriver and uphill, past a series of rapids on the Sturgeon-Weir River. Small wonder that they chose to go by dogsled when the rivers were frozen, preferably in March or November.

Rice decided to trade the plough for a pick and join the stampede too. She read everything she could find about minerals and pored over rock samples, readying herself for a new career as a prospector. Her first prospecting trip was in March 1913. She hired an Aboriginal guide with sled dogs. They mushed northwest through virgin forests to Beaver/Amisk Lake, on to Reindeer Lake, and all the way to Brochet, a distance of 452 kilometres.[8] Despite the rigours of the trip, she wore her hair and skirts primly long to avoid shocking her guide or the Hudson Bay factor at Amisk Lake.

Alone in the Bush

On her return, Rice spent the winter of 1913-14 alone with her dogs, living six kilometres from The Pas.[9] Her first lone prospecting trip was in 1914 when she set out by dogsled to the Scoopin' Rapids about 160 kilometres north of The Pas on the Sturgeon-Weir River.[10] She poked around in the rocks a bit and staked a claim. A literary friend in Chicago grubstaked her first venture in mining. In return she made notes and pictures of her wilderness excursions.

While she learned the ropes as a prospector, Rice sustained herself by trapping for food and pelts. The furs she brought in fetched enough cash to pay for materials for a log cabin complete with a bathtub, said to be the first in the district.

When Rice emerged from the woods in the fall of 1914 she learned there was a war going on in Europe. A letter from her mother announced that her brother Lincoln had enlisted on September 22, shortly after Britain and its Empire became embroiled in the war. He shipped out with the 3rd Battalion, Canadian Expeditionary Force.[11] Many local prospectors also joined the exodus to the front. Rice wrangled with the government for a while about gaining title to the land, but rules were rules, and single women without children weren't eligible. (At war's end Lincoln came back and finished proving up the land, obtaining title in 1918, but later returned to St. Marys.)

Like Ginger Rogers, who as they say did everything Fred Astaire did but on high heels and backwards, Rice fulfilled the roles that women everywhere did, only more so. When she was at home, she kept a garden. Not only did she can her own food, she killed her own game and dressed the meat and hides herself. She was also adept with a hammer.

In the wilderness Rice staked her own claims and hacked away at them to disclose mineral traces. Her vigorous lifestyle probably built muscles, but she was not a brawny Amazon type. Some things she could not do. She relied on men to do the tasks that required brute strength or practical skills she lacked. Her biographer, Helen Duncan, has her build her cabin on her own, but Rice told an interviewer later that she had hired men to build it.

On a long portage, if she couldn't carry her equipment, she patiently waited for a man to come along. Her canoe alone weighed almost fifty kilograms (one hundred pounds) and her pack about forty (seventy-five pounds). She relied much on Aboriginal packers to help her, and formed close relationships with some of them and their families.

A ROOMMATE FOR KATHLEEN

Living alone in the bush was a domestic situation that spooked even seasoned prospectors. Months of solitude brought the risk of becoming "bushed," and life in the northern wilds entailed real hazards, especially in winter. Clearly there were advantages to partnerships, mainly mutual support and sharing of tasks. She was on the lookout for a partner.

Probably in early 1914 she crossed paths with prospector Dick Woosey, although she may have met him earlier.[12] He was looking for a partner too. Which of the two suggested that they team up is not clear as she didn't appreciate men making unwelcome advances, but Rice moved into Woosey's cabin at Chisel Lake further to the east. On May 15, 1914, they signed a contract defining their union as a business partnership, according to Duncan.

A veteran of the Boer War, Woosey had served with the 18th Hussars, a British cavalry regiment later known as Queen Mary's Own that had fought at Waterloo, Balaclava, Mons, India, and South Africa. He had brought his wife and child to Canada, but as soon as they landed at Halifax she balked at the idea of a backwoods life, returned to England, and that was the end of that.

Kathleen Rice (middle) with the Kobar sisters. – *Photo 94.40.1, courtesy of the Sam Waller Museum, The Pas.*

Woosey was a burly, squat figure at five foot seven (170 cm) – Rice was six feet (180 cm) – with coarse black hair and a dusky complexion. He was garrulous, companionable, and an adroit horseman with practical skills honed in the army. Some say he had a sensitive streak, more sensitive than she. No matter how far away she was, whenever Rice was caught up in some scrape, he'd appear like a white knight in the nick of time to rescue her.

Duncan's 1984 book *Kate Rice: Prospector* is a fictionalized biography, constructing plausible or probable scenarios and dates and imagined conversations, though contemporary news accounts and Rice's own writings and interviews tell quite a different story.[13] However, by changing names to avoid lawsuits, Duncan could tell a tale of skulduggery in the mining industry.

Duncan also uncloaked the locally known "secret" that Rice and Woosey were living together. She thought that the pair shared the same cabin for decades in a platonic relationship, but others scoff at the notion.

Were they lovers or not? There was certainly a fiercely protective bond between them, especially on Woosey's part, but there were no children. Perhaps Rice didn't even fancy men, or squelched her sex drive. Some local prospectors and mining engineers *did* see the two as "shacked up."[14] Woosey had a wife somewhere in England, and divorce was a tremendous hurdle in Canada at that time. Common-law bonds caused tongues to wag, and her living arrangements would have upset her parents, especially her society mother.

In a telling revelation, when asked by a reporter if she ever thought of marriage, Rice replied, "All the time," and then hastily added that she thought more about business. Asked, "Are you absolutely on your own; no partner or anybody to go out in the wilds with you?" she smiled coyly and said, "Of course I am on my own. I swing on my own gate, absolutely."[15] She did not admit to sharing her cabin with a man, much less her bed. The reporter claimed she had no interest in men except as miners and prospectors. Rice was living with Woosey at the time, though, so she hardly needed another.

In 1917 or 1918 Rice ventured further northeast to Wekusko Lake. At some point, to escape the new settlement of Herb Lake invading the east-

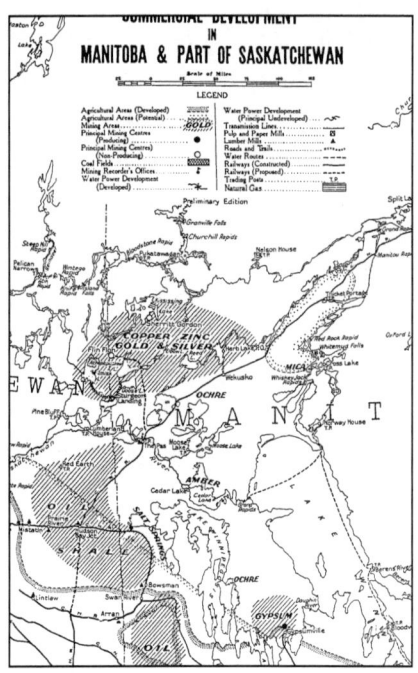

Map showing mineral occurrences in northern Manitoba, Dept. of the Interior, 1929. – *Courtesy of Archives of Manitoba.*

ern lakeshore, she (and probably Woosey) moved onto the island on the lake. It was later renamed Rice Island. In 1920 she staked a claim on her island and clung stubbornly to it, though nothing panned out officially until 1928. According to local legend, one day while standing on the shore of Wekusko/ Herb Lake, Rice saw a rainbow pointing to a spot on her island. She drilled at that very spot and sent in samples from it to be assayed. While waiting for the assayer's report she hired ten men who dug, drilled, and dynamited. The report came back with thrilling news: her samples contained "paying quantities" of copper pyrites, a bonanza for her because the price of copper had skyrocketed due to wartime demands.

Starting July 1928, a flurry of headlines appeared in North American newspapers noting the rich strike made by this plucky woman prospector on a faraway island. She also found significant deposits of nickel, sulphides, and zinc, and showings of vanadium and even gold.[16] (Rice wasn't much interested in gold. She left that to Woosey, who had discovered gold on the shores of Wekusko Lake possibly as early as 1913, sparking a mini gold rush.[17]) Mining engineers arrived to talk to her. Exaggerated rumours flitted around the mining community about the value of her claims, and she became an overnight celebrity when she returned to visit her parents.

Rice was generous with her tributes regarding help she received from Aboriginal people. Of that first mining foray in 1913, she said her Aboriginal guide did everything. Natives of the area called her *Mooniasquao,* meaning "white woman." Some of them said she was the best white trapper they knew. Among her friends was Mrs. Custer, a woman of Aboriginal descent with whom she communicated non-verbally. The Custers invited her to join them and their friends by the clay fireplace in their log cabin to hear the elders tell their ancient stories.

In 1928 Rice was about forty-five but still handsome. By 1934 other women were studying geology, but Rice was the only woman in Manitoba who was actually out in the wilds working as a prospector.[18] Reports of her doings exclaimed over the novelty of a gun-toting woman prospector in pants, thriving in the wilderness winter and summer, alone with her dogs named Sandy, June, Ruddy, and Douglas. The reports never mentioned the man who shared her cabin. Her unwomanly garments startled onlookers. In the late 1920s, even in the remote northern woods, respectable women were expected to dress and behave in a more seemly way.

RICE RUNS THE RAPIDS

One of her most famous adventures was a hair-raising canoe trip in 1928 down the Sturgeon-Weir, the river the French called *Maligne* (wicked) because of its rapids. In Duncan's book she did it alone. In reality she did it under the watchful supervision of an expert guide, a Mr. MacDonald, to avoid the calamities suffered by tenderfoot prospectors over the years: lost equipment, shattered canoes, near drownings. She described her breathtaking trip in a *Star Weekly* article a year later.[19]

That autumn of 1928 Rice had gone to check out claims she had staked out at Scoopin' Rapids years earlier, between Amisk Lake and Maligne Lake. She had tarried too long at an Indian encampment. Winter was settling in. To get back to her home cabin required a canoe trip of about 160 kilometres down the Sturgeon-Weir River to the Saskatchewan and on to The Pas. From there she would take the Hudson Bay Railway to Herb Lake. At the ghost town of Beaver Lake she persuaded its only resident Mr. MacDonald, to guide her down the dangerous river. (Nowadays, white water canoeists swoop down that river more easily using plastic canoes that regain their shape after colliding with rocks and act like slippery toboggans in shallow places, with special hulls and skid plates to skim over the cheese-grater river bottom of limestone rock. Rice's little canoe, The Duckling, was clunky and awkward by comparison.[20])

The worst section of the trip was between Beaver/Amisk Lake and Sturgeon Landing, along what Alexander Mackenzie, and Rice, called "an almost continuous rapid." It drops steeply at 0.75 metres per kilometre (4 feet per mile). When they reached the Crooked Rapids, MacDonald insisted on piloting both of their canoes while she watched from shore as he expertly guided the craft in its descent along a smooth channel between jutting boulders on either side. The two continued on for ten or twelve hours, running the rapids until they reached the worst obstacle, the Rat Rapids above Sturgeon Landing (although she did not mention them by name). This time he gave her a choice, and she chose to challenge the famous torrent that had supposedly overwhelmed many white men. Rushing waters gathering force over fifty kilometres descended on those rapids, roared around two right-angle bends, and finally splayed out in the broad mouth that entered the lake. She made it. As she glided alongside MacDonald's canoe below the rapid, he asked how much water she had taken aboard and seemed almost aggrieved when she reported none. Rice felt a little smug, for he had earlier sneered at her canoeing abilities.

At Sturgeon Landing, she reloaded her goods into The Duckling and paddled on alone. She passed through sleet storms that soaked her and blizzards of snow, camping in the snow-muffled forest or stopping to refuel her shivering body at Cree settlements along the way. Later on that trip, as her canoe was swept along by the current of the Saskatchewan and then the Tearing River, floating ice cakes formed around her. Rice had not seen before that annual spectacle of ice floes surging down the river just before freeze-up. Sometimes she was trapped in an ice jam; sometimes she circled slowly in a whirlpool. She discovered that her canoe could ride the "ribbons of ice" moving with the current between solid patches, and that was how she made it back.

FACING THE WILD THINGS

Another escapade involved four-legged beings. On a trip in mid-October 1928, she did not make it back to her base camp by nightfall and had to camp overnight in the wilderness. Glimpsing the grey shapes of wolves lurking in the woods nearby, she lit a fire to keep them at bay. When a bull moose appeared she realized that although it could be dangerous, it could also protect her from the wolves, for even wolves feared an angry bull moose. She raced to a hollow formed by protruding tree roots and took shelter there for the night, making small scrabbling noises to keep the moose intrigued enough to linger nearby until morning.

Publishers wooed Rice for memoirs of her astonishing life. She was too busy, she said – she would do it when she grew old. A *Star Weekly* account of her 1928 adventures was the closest she came to autobiography, aside from a nearly illegible diary that reveals little about herself.[21] Not that she was averse to writing. In her leisure hours Rice read her books, listened to the radio, and wrote. Seemingly of a poetic nature despite her rugged occupation, she would sit and gaze at the sky, admiring the northern lights. Her somewhat scholarly musings were published in such prestigious journals as the *Journal of the Royal Astronomical Society of Canada*, which carried her article on nature's heavenly light show.[22]

FAMILY VISITS

Woosey no doubt made himself scarce when Rice's father came to visit. Mr. Rice came at least once, to try to persuade her to come back to Ontario to live a conventional life. Her answer was no. After her father died in 1933, her seventy-six year old mother braved the wilds to visit her daughter's rustic island home, supposedly in 1939. Mother and daughter chartered a plane and flew over Churchill. Two years after that aerial jaunt her mother died.

Meanwhile the Wekusko Lake area had mushroomed into a thriving community. By 1929 steam-powered locomotives roared by a nearby community, Wekusko, south of the Herb Lake settlement; the steel had almost reached Hudson Bay.[23] The trains were their only link with the world until bush planes began droning into the remote settlement every week in the mid-thirties. Rice and Woosey could mush forty kilometres across the ice to Mile 18 at Wekusko and take the Hudson Bay Railway to The Pas. It connected with the CNR, their passport to the rest of Canada.

According to Duncan, Woosey was an innocent in the world of mining exploration and was bilked out of his rich find, the Kiski Mines, by swindlers. Supposedly the mining certificates were "street-type" with no names assigned, and a scam artist juggled the certificates into a different file. Whatever the true story, rights to the property were indeed contested.

In 1916 his Kiski gold mine had been swallowed up by a mining company that later merged with a large mining concern in 1920.[24] "The partners are said to have refused $250,000.00 in cash and shares for the property, in the belief it was worth much more," according to the Snow Lake website (a community that sprang up nearby). When Woosey died in 1941 the pair still had not been paid for their property. It is believed Rice received $23,000.00 for her share. Duncan depicts Woosey's fatal heart attack being brought on by the legal scrap over ownership of the mining certificates. Dick collapsed in the barber's chair at The Pas, and was buried in the town cemetery.

RICE SOLDIERS ON

Rice had lived alone in the bush before and she could do it again. She stayed alone in her cabin for years. She could have moved to Herb Lake, where even in 1928 there were other European women in the district: the assistant postmaster, school teachers, storekeepers' wives, and a soldier's wife. The townies called her "The Lady of the Island." (By the 1950s Herb Lake had become a ghost town.)

Once in a while Rice went to Toronto, such as in 1943 when she had all her teeth pulled and dentures fitted.[25] Eventually she began to think she was bushed, that peculiar malady of long-isolated trappers and prospectors. Convinced she was going insane, she buried her small mining fortune (estimated at $23,000 to $45,000) in the northern wilds and left.[26] She turned up at a mental institution in Brandon, Manitoba, and announced that she was insane. She was not mad, but she did not return to the north. Kathleen Rice died in 1963 (a year after her only sibling, Lt.-Col. G. D. L. Rice of St. Marys) at the age of eighty in a nursing home in Minnedosa. She was buried there.

Several geographical features in northern Manitoba bear the name of Woosey or Rice. Rice Island and Woosey Island nestle close to each other in Wekusko Lake, their closeness a symbol of two enigmatic lives spent together in the northern wilds.

James smouldering good looks inspired movie offers, which he disdained.
– *courtesy National Cowboy and Western Heritage Museum, Oklahoma City, OK.*

ERNEST DUFAULT
alias WILL JAMES
Cowboy Hero and Impostor

Will James was a lone wolf, a vagabond, a bronco-buster, an artist, a story-teller, a daredevil, and even a cattle rustler, but at heart he was just a cowboy. His rise to glory involved a brazen hoax that fooled fans around the world and even his wife.

Lean, wiry, and bow-legged, at about five foot eight (173 centimetres) and weighing a trim 135 pounds (61 kilograms), he was blessed with brooding good looks. With his smouldering brown eyes, thick dark hair, and Grecian profile he could have been a movie star. He spurned the offer of a movie career in favour of his other great passion – art – but it was his gift as a raconteur that propelled him all the way to Hollywood and New York and landed him among the movie stars of his day. Kids idolized him; adults thought he was a hero.

In his autobiography, *Lone Cowboy*, Will James wrote that his parents were of mostly Scottish descent, that his father was a Texan and his mother a Californian with traces of Spanish blood. He claimed to have been born in Montana while his parents were trekking north to Canada, and that they remained in Montana after his birth. His mother died of the flu when he was one. His broken-hearted father was gored by a steer when Will was four. The dying father entrusted his son to the Métis trapper Jean Beaupré (Bopy for short), who obligingly took the boy with him as he criss-crossed the northern bush country in western Canada, always one step ahead of the law.

In this imagined childhood his boy-self was often left alone in rustic cabins while Bopy scoured the woods for food or trapped furs. The boy entertained himself by drawing, inspired by illustrated magazines that just happened to be lying around. (James's early drawings do show this influence; his women, in particular, mirror fashions in illustration at the time). This frontier life allowed the boy to romp with the horses he loved. He boosted his survival skills as he fearlessly confronted wolves, grizzly bears, snakes, and other aggressive wildlife.

Finally one spring, the old man accidentally drowned in a swollen prairie river. Will, abandoned once more, began his apprenticeship as a cowboy, drifting from ranch to ranch, moving from low-status jobs like "camp flunky," "night hawk," and "wrangatang" to become a top-notch cowboy and broncobuster.

At this point in his memoir, James shakes himself out of this fantasy world into reality. Cannily, he avoided mentioning dates or places, so that his footprints were difficult to track. His story was believed by everyone, even his wife and close friends, for nearly a quarter century after his early death.

Biographer Anthony Amaral was the first to stumble on the truth. In 1967, when he published his findings in *Will James, the Gilt-Edged Cowboy*, the truth about James vibrated through the American literary world. He had sniffed out James's will amongst the court records of Yellowstone County, Montana. In an act of amazing cheek, or else in an alcoholic stupor, James had left his estate to his other self, Ernest Dufault.[1] Even nearing his death, he was still afraid people would find out he was an impostor, not a Montana-born cowboy but a Quebecois city slicker.

THE REAL STORY

Gradually Amaral pieced together the real story. Will James was born Joseph Ernest Nephthali Dufault on June 6, 1892, the son of Jean Baptiste and Josephine[2] Dufault in St-Nazaire d'Acton, a village in the St. Lawrence River Valley in Quebec. Ernest was the second of six children, three girls and three boys. His uncle Napoleon had a farm nearby. As early as four years old, Ernest began sketching horses, cattle, and dogs. At the turn of the century, the family moved to Montreal, then moved several more times, and finally settled for a while in suburban St. Hyacinthe, where his father ran a boarding house called the Hôtel Union in 1906.

Métis trappers who stayed at the Hôtel Union regaled young Ernest (a.k.a Will) with stories of their adventures in the northern bush. He mentally stashed away those tales, unpacking them years later for his Bopy story.

When Buffalo Bill's Wild West Show came to Montreal, young Ernest was spellbound. Already smitten with horses, he was further beguiled by the romance of the Old West. In 1907, at the age of fifteen, he left home and took the train to Regina with ten dollars in his pocket.

Naturally, growing up in Quebec, Dufault spoke French, not English. The shift to the mainly English-speaking West must have been wrenching for him, like moving to a foreign country. Although there had long been Quebec cowhands in the West, in the ethnic patchwork of cowboy culture the common language was English. There were pockets of French communities in southern Saskatchewan that were probably a comfortable retreat for him as he grappled with a new language. Around this time he tried on a few different English names. He may have invented his "Bopy" past then as well, to account for his French accent.

Years later, to his mother's distress, he destroyed the telltale family papers that proved his real origins, but some clues still mark his trail in western Canada. One family letter indicates his first home in the West may have been in Manitoba on the farm of a family named Goodrich. In 1910 he was likely working on the John Moir ranch near the Cypress Hills.[3] In 1995 Moir's son remembered relatives reminiscing about the young French Canadian who drew all over the cook's tent.[4]

In 1909 or 1910 Dufault made a trip home to Quebec to see his family. He also sent a postcard, postmarked September 1911, from Kelvinhurst, Saskatchewan, south of Maple Creek, near Vidora. Kelvinhurst was a post office that existed only from 1910 to 1914. Dufault wrote in French on the postcard that he was working for the 76 Cattle Company. That was the popular name for large herds of livestock imported from the United States; it was not the legal name of a company. The "76" herd was scattered on large tracts of land along the CPR line from Swift Current west into Alberta.[5] Dufault was a line rider on the "76" ranch at Gull Lake, and perhaps other "76" ranches.

He may also have worked at the well-known Turkey Track ranch at Hallonquist, and other ranches at Wood Mountain and in the Cypress Hills area.[6] The vast ranches were shrinking as grain farming in the area increased.[7] According to historian Bill Waiser, James also started a ranch in the Cypress Hills, near Ravenscrag, Saskatchewan. "Don't Fence Me In" could have been James's theme song; he mourned the passing of the fenceless range lands and felt cooped up in cities.

HOMESTEADING

In the summer of 1911 Dufault applied for a homestead and a preemption,[8] signing the application under his new moniker of William R. James, perhaps a more fitting name for a cowboy. His land was located near the village of Val Marie on the south side of the White Mud (Frenchman) River in the Gergovia district[9] in an area now part of Grasslands National Park in southern Saskatchewan. James wrote in *Lone Cowboy* that it took him about a month to build a shack out of willow branches, mud, and grass on the bank of a creek flowing through his property. He lived on this homestead only a few months.

Several decades later, when community histories of the area were written, Will James still lingered in the popular memory. One old-timer wrote: "The most famous cowboy of the '76' was undoubtedly Will James...a line rider for the '76'. He and his beloved Smoky roamed over our hills, just when the settlers were starting to arrive."[10]

Then, in late 1911, something happened, and abruptly James had to vamoose across the border. Perhaps he actually did kill a man in a barroom brawl, and maybe he was thrown in the clink for a spell, as he related in *Lone Cowboy*. James is said to have mumbled drunkenly years later that he had been jailed in Canada and had escaped by the chancy and improbable tactic of setting fire to the log enclosure.

Will James spent the winter of 1911 on the John Moir Ranch at Cypress Hills, Sask., when this photo was taken. – *Photo NA-862 courtesy of Glenbow Museum and Archives, Calgary.*

The way he told it in *Lone Cowboy* suggests he was cooped up in one of several North West Mounted Police posts strung like beads along Saskatchewan and Alberta trails. But so far no proof has emerged that he was involved in a murder in Saskatchewan, at least under the names Will James, Ernest Dufault, C. R. Jackson, or any of the other aliases he adopted before settling on his final name. More likely he did not kill anyone but was held briefly as a suspect in the case; if he had been convicted his name would appear in homicide records.

French-Canadian filmmaker Jacques Godbout thought young

Dufault ran afoul of the Mounties in Calgary. Accused of murder in a fracas in a Calgary saloon, the young cowpoke fled to Montana, not to escape the law, but because he was piqued at the Mounties for his unjust arrest, Godbout suggests.[11]

Wherever it was, in that jail Will felt like a wild horse caged in a corral. In a 1931 story his character, Bill, feels such remorse for capturing a band of wild horses he releases them, although he could sell them for a hefty sum. A black stallion was the last to gallop away.[12] A black stallion often appears in his books as a symbol of freedom.

Abandoning his cozy sod-roofed shack at Val Marie, he left to live in the United States, probably in late 1911, after trading his French identity for a new English-speaking self. For a while he roamed the West alone, working as an itinerant cowboy. Then he fell in with a band of cowpokes, including the rascal Lew Hackberry, who led him astray on a cattle-rustling caper. Hackberry escaped, but James was caught. James was eventually convicted of grand larceny and sentenced to Nevada State Penitentiary in Carson City.

While awaiting trial James was penned up in Ely, Nevada, where prison officials discovered his riding talents. He was given the plum job of exercising the horses stabled there. When he wasn't doing that, he whiled away the hours in his cell practising his drawing. His finely crafted sketches of horses and cowboys (who looked like him) were praised by his jailers and wowed the local press.

Soon after he was sprung from prison on April 11, 1916, James signed on for a bronco-busting job at the Rickey Ranch in Bridgeport, California. At the ranch's winter range

James's cowboy depictions tended to mirror his own Western image. – *courtesy National Cowboy and Heritage Museum, Oklahoma City, OK.*

near Carson City, a violent argument with a rebellious horse ended in damage to his jaw, and he headed off to Hollywood for dental repairs.

There he ran into Sam Long, who got him a job as a movie extra at the Clarence Jones Stables. Later James was hired on at the Thomas Ince Studios. Despite all the tinsel and glamour of Hollywood, James had no intention of becoming an actor. He jeered at movie versions of cowboy life. There was enough uproar in a cowboy's real life, he thought – no need to embellish it with phoney shoot-'em-up violence.

Longing for the open range again, Will rambled for two years around the West on horseback. He drifted north to Canada in 1917, where he roamed the rodeo circuit with Lloyd Garrison, Bob Stadley, "Calgary Red," and "Sleepy" Emerson, riding in the bronco-

Elmer Freel, Will James and Fred Conradt (the One-Elevens) in 1919. – *Photo 2270/J, courtesy of Special Collections Department, University of Nevada - Reno.*

busting events at Taber, Hardisty, and Medicine Hat, Alberta, and Moose Jaw, Saskatchewan. In Medicine Hat, the foursome staged a rollicking public riding display in the street.

Among his pals, James was known as "Bullshit Bill." His talents as a storyteller who laced his stories with invention had already surfaced.

After another fateful run-in with an outlaw horse, and suffering dizzy spells from internal injuries, James knew his days as a broncobuster were numbered. Since his drawings were such a hit, he thought he might switch careers and become a cowboy artist. In the winter of 1917-18 he visited the famous western artist Charles Russell in Great Falls, Montana, but was disappointed by Russell's lukewarm reception.

There was a war going on, however, and the feds were looking for him, so he enlisted. From May 1918 to February 1919 James served as a mounted scout and orderly with the 21st Infantry Regiment stationed near San Diego, "taking the rough off horses."

After his discharge in February 1919, he trotted off to Reno. There he looked up a cowpoke he knew, Fred Conradt, who became a lifelong chum. James began to hang out at the Conradt house, attracted by Fred's strikingly pretty fifteen-year-old sister, Alice. At that point James was a greenhorn when it came to women. He even compared them to horses, describing girls in Hollywood as "....some nice ones, too, of all styles, from running to draft types."[13]

James, Fred Conradt, and another friend, Elmer Freel, calling themselves the One-Elevens, cooked up the idea of staging a bronco-busting exhibition, but during a practice session James was tossed onto a railway track by a disgruntled horse named Happy. James ended up in hospital with a torn scalp and a concussion. A fellow patient, impressed with his drawing, gave him a letter of introduction to an editor at *Sunset Magazine*. While his body was mending, James stayed at the Conradt home, where things began to sizzle with Alice. She encouraged him to take formal art training.

Cowboy Artist

His father had sent him to art school as a teenager, but the young Dufault had rebelled at the discipline of drawing from models. James's way of drawing was intuitive. He instinctively recorded his vivid mental images on paper, his artful lines flowing into powerful sketches of horses in action. In 1919, egged on by Alice Conradt, he registered for evening art classes at the California School of Fine Arts in San Francisco. But it wasn't his scene. Believing that formal classes would ruin his free-spirited drawing style, he dropped out of art school.

It was said that his bucking horses seem to "explode from the page." In the absence of modern high-speed cameras, he could only freeze that action from his own memory pictures. He knew every muscle and sinew, every twist and turn of a bucking horse, and sketched them swiftly and masterfully. The cliché about a cowboy's first love being his horse fitted him exactly. So profound was his identification with horses that he once drew himself as a centaur looking at itself in a mirror.

Before leaving the Conradt household in San Francisco, James sold some drawings to the associate editor at *Sunset Magazine*, launching a series of sketches in the magazine in January 1920. Then he moved to a nearby art colony at Sausalito. He sent a sketch to Charlie Russell, and this time the famous artist cheered him on.

His relationship with Alice was rosy too. On July 7, 1920, Will James and Alice Conradt were married at Reno. He was twenty-eight, she sixteen. They got by on a skimpy income as James struggled to become known as an artist. He sent off a batch of drawings to three New York publishers. They were rejected, so he took a job tending stock on an Arizona ranch, where he and Alice lived in a spartan one-room cabin. Alice, who was frightened of spiders, snakes, scorpions, and other crawling beings, felt isolated but hid her misery.

In 1921 the couple left for Santa Fe, New Mexico, another artists' haven. There they spent several idyllic months, and James began marketing his drawings to tourists and local ranchers. James struck up a friendship with an artist who got him a job on the ranch belonging to his brother, Ed Springer. Alice returned to Reno, and James worked and drew, papering the bunkhouse with his pictures.

Will James and his wife Alice at Washoe Valley Cabin. – *Photo 2270/T, courtesy of Special Collections Department, University of Nevada - Reno.*

Will James on his favourite seat – a western saddle. – *courtesy National Cowboy and Western Heritage Museum, Oklahoma City, OK.*

COWBOY AUTHOR

That year, in a chance encounter at the Ed Springer ranch in Cimarron where he was working, two eminent visitors offered to pay his fees to art school, and Burton Twichell, Dean of Students at Yale University, offered him a scholarship to study art. James took off for Connecticut but didn't last long at that school either. Again he chucked it all to pursue his own drawing style.

When publication of his illustrations brought in only a miserly living, Alice, who recognized James's creative talents as a storyteller, spurred him to his first writing efforts. Publishers may have been tepid about his sketches, but when the drawings were animated by his colourful, drawling prose, they quickly became a hot commodity. His first big break came in 1923 when Scribner's in New York began printing his illustrated essays and stories. James was hurled into a literary firmament that included such stars as Ernest Hemingway and F. Scott Fitzgerald.

The mid-twenties were fairly idyllic for Will and Alice. In 1923, *Smoky the Cowhorse*[14] won the prestigious Newbery Medal for children's literature. He became a sudden celebrity, and "rode horseback down Madison Avenue in 1928 as the star attraction in a gala parade that opened the New York rodeo. To New Yorkers, Will James was the quintessential cowboy, American born and bred."[15] Another time he trotted on horseback into a posh hotel lobby in New York and shot at the lights, thus spawning a certain dubious tradition in cowboy movies. He indulged in similar escapades in Texas, Hollywood, and Montana.

James's books were praised by critics for their fresh, folksy style, although some hooted at his fractured grammar. Artfully, he laid it on thick (he was quite capable of writing nearly correct English, as many of his letters show). He carried around a notebook in which he recorded the picturesque phrases that real cowboys used, and his prose bubbled with pungent images. He may have been the first to coin the expression "think tank," which for him meant a pony's brain.

For about two years Will and Alice led a gypsy life, always on the move. Finally they bought their dream ranch in the foothills of Pryor, Montana, south of Billings. They called it the Rocking R, the name of a ranch in one of James's novels. James bought a classy car, a 1920 Pierce Arrow. He didn't know how to drive, but that didn't faze him. He eased himself behind the wheel of his shiny new horseless carriage, with his wife gamely by his side. The motor idling, he located reverse gear and jerkily let out the clutch. The car hurtled backward across the street and crashed into a telephone pole. The engine stalled. Ashen-faced, Will turned to Alice, who was equally shaken. "God a-mighty!" he gasped. "I think I spurred it too hard."[16]

But skyrocketing success brought trouble. To pay for the ranch, he had to churn out books and stories at a gruelling pace. He and Alice dashed around to rodeos, parties, and book-signing engagements, and he was drawn into a boozy lifestyle he had learned when he and his young cowboy pals had flocked into town on weekends. In 1929, James published his novel *Sand*, about a drunken city dude who redeems his life, moves out west to Montana, gentles a wild stallion, and wins the girl. The reverse parallel to James's life was ironic. Although on the surface he was sailing smoothly, in reality he was sinking under his burdens. Alice, fed up with his binges, was about to stop being his lifeboat.

In October 1929 the stock market crashed. Ignoring financial advice from his publisher, James impulsively bought another 240 acres to add to his acreage at the Rocking R Ranch. In November 1929 he travelled to New York without Alice and disappeared on a toot. Alice tracked him down at a dude ranch in San Antonio, Texas. Contrite after he sobered up, he suggested she leave him. She reminded him of their plans to work on his autobiography together. So they left together for San Francisco, and in 1930 he published his famous book *Lone Cowboy*. Oddly, she had to prompt him to mention their courtship and marriage, and he only gave it a few lines.

Despite his personal miseries, James's writing career was still booming. In 1932 Fox Studios bought the rights to *Smoky*, and he sold *Lone Cowboy* to Paramount. When the couple moved to Hollywood, James frolicked amongst such celebrities as Bing Crosby, Jimmy Durante, Chill Wills, and Wallace Beery.[17] He too became a celebrity, cruising around in his sleek black convertible.

Three movies were made about the spunky little cow horse Smoky – in 1933, 1946, and 1966 – based on his best-seller *Smoky the Cowhorse*. One starred Fred MacMurray, Anne Baxter, and Burl Ives. James was offered a movie role as narrator in the 1933 version. He did appear briefly in it, but in an alcoholic fog he flubbed his lines so badly they had to dub in another actor's voice.

In 1934 James made one last trip home to Quebec to visit his family, on the sly and without Alice because she knew nothing of his French-Canadian origins. Probably he needed the escape, as their stormy relationship was draining them both.

After his disgraceful drunken antics he'd wring his hands and cry and beg forgiveness. Submissive to him at first as a teenage bride, as Alice matured she became the strong one. She groped along the collapsing bridge that was their marriage, trying to prop up the crumbling piers of love and light, joy and passion that had sustained them. Her instincts told her it was useless, but her mother insisted. Divorce was unthinkable in those days.

In 1935, addled by liquor, James sold the ranch and livestock for one thousand dollars. Quick action by a lawyer snatched back the ranch, but the livestock were lost. Alice gave up on their marriage for good.

Late in 1936 James left his dream ranch after losing it to creditors. He moved into a basement study provided by his friends Earl and Eleanor Snook, owners of the Snook Art Company in Billings. "Soon after James' world had shattered beneath him, Earl found his true identity through some letters to James from his brother Auguste. James swore Earl to secrecy...."[18] Earl kept that vow, and the secret remained buried until 1967 when Amaral unearthed the courthouse records.

In early 1937, James smashed up a car in Billings, Montana. On a charge of drunk driving, he was ordered to dry out at the Presbyterian Hospital for Inebriates in Warmsprings, Montana. In July 1937, the James's divorce settlement was finalized, giving Alice part of their property.

In the summer of 1942, Alice visited him in Hollywood and beheld a wasted man. On August 28, 1942, he collapsed and was taken to Hollywood Presbyterian Hospital, where on September 3, 1942, at just fifty years old, Will James died of cirrhosis of the liver and kidney failure, the physical legacy of chronic alcoholism. His ashes were flung out of an airplane, at his request, over the Montana ranchlands.

Despite his tragic end, Will James left a legacy of books and drawings that continues to delight horse lovers and cowboy fans. And like that other famous impostor Grey Owl, a.k.a. Archie Belaney, James got away with his hoax. Furthermore, James could be the only man who ever bequeathed his estate to himself. Perhaps he did so knowing that it would be traced back to his Montreal family, and that his brother would sort it out in court (which he did), but it suggests an impudent sense of humour.

As a Medicine Hat admirer wrote, though Will James is remembered as an American, Canadians should reclaim Will James as our own cultural icon.[19]

Charlie Parmer – *Photo LH 3581, courtesy of the Saskatoon Public Library Local History Room.*

CHARLIE PARMER
Notorious Outlaw or Faker?

Untamed as a wolf, a bizarre figure shuffled through the dirt roads of Dundurn, Saskatchewan in the early years of the twentieth century, trailing his dubious past behind him. His hair was long and unkempt, his beard matted, his clothes scruffy and unclean, and he probably reeked. He carried a gun.

Charles Augustus Parmer seems like a character out of a Hollywood western, not an ordinary homesteader quietly raising livestock near the sleepy town south of Saskatoon. Where did he come from, and what secrets was he hiding? People wondered then, and they still do. It is anybody's guess whether the legends about this bizarre character are true.

Overcome with curiosity, one day in 1932 an anonymous newspaper reporter and an unnamed university professor from Saskatoon trekked out to the old man's homestead. (The professor, it turns out, may have been the eminent Grant MacEwan, later lieutenant-governor of Alberta.[1]) The old man said he was born in Brookfield, Ohio, on March 13, 1839. His father moved to a farm in Pennsylvania, where Charles helped clear 360 acres. Asked if he fought in the American Civil War that raged in the United States between 1861 and 1865, he replied, "Naw, I came over to Canady and got a substitute. I got substitutes for a lot of my neighbours that were drafted."[2]

Parmer admitted having killed two cattle rustlers, but there were five notches filed into the back strap of the pistol butt of his .44 six-shooter.[3] Some think he fought in the Civil War, although there is no proof. At least one writer[4] claimed that during the war Charlie Parmer fought with the infamous gang led by William Clarke Quantrill, a group known for Confederate guerrilla warfare. No proof has been found to prove that claim either.

JESSE JAMES AND BUFFALO BILL

Allen Parmer, said to be Charlie's brother, appears on the roster of men who were members of the Quantrill gang.[5] So does a man named Isaac Parmer. But Charlie does not. Either Charlie did not consider their guerrilla activities as war service, or he did not wish to speak of it, or the stories about him are untrue. The Quantrill gang raided communities throughout Missouri and Kansas and battled Union troops. Even if Charlie didn't ride with the Quantrill gang, they were clearly in his neck of the woods when he was in his twenties.

Perhaps after the Civil War Parmer took part in bank raids and train robberies with the infamous James gang. Perhaps not. Before Jesse and Frank James formed their own gang they were guerrilla fighters in the war, as members of the Anderson gang. Records show that an Allen Parmer married Jesse James's sister Susan.[6] If this Allen Parmer was Charlie's brother, Charlie would likely have bumped into the famous outlaw one way or the other. So far no *proven* link between Charlie and the James brothers has been found, but it all sounds plausible.

Gripped by a fascination with the strange old man, Dundurn history buffs went searching for answers. They mined the sands of memory and myth, panning out nuggets of fact. Then local farmer Harvey Mawson alloyed them into something more solid. In 1998 the Wilson Museum published Mawson's slim anthology, *Fast Gun*.[7]

In a 1932 interview, Charlie admitted that he knew James, but he did not admit to any bank robberies. Nor did he deny it. Of course, if he were a fugitive from gun-battles and bank heists in the American Midwest, why would he want to stir up the Mounties by publicly admitting he was a bank robber?

Harry Friesen, one of the founders of the Wilson Museum in Dundurn, was only six when Charlie Parmer died. The Friesen family's farm adjoined the Parmer homestead. Harry ran into the elder Parmer only once in a while. He did know Parmer's son, Earl, who admired and respected his father and was fairly close-mouthed about his dad's exploits. The two southerners did not exactly fit into the community, but several neighbours in the area knew and liked the fierce-looking old man. Some of those who crossed the elder Parmer faced the barrel of his guns, although no one in the area was actually shot by a Parmer bullet.

In the 1932 interview, the old man was ninety-three. He was a "short thickset figure with a tobacco-stained grey beard, wearing a cowboy hat." One of two photographs that survive shows a grizzled old man with beard that brushed his chest. The other shows the aged Parmer standing in front of his rickety shack, apparently clutching a rifle. In 1932, Parmer still had an arsenal of weapons, one a gun some say was used in the Civil War.

Parmer did boast that he had worked with Buffalo Bill Cody and that he had shot two men. As he remembered it, he got into a brawl in Pennsylvania, was arrested, skipped bail, and headed for the Wild West to join the outlaw Jesse James. But he wasn't *bad* enough to be a bandit, James told him, because he hadn't killed anyone yet. So James sent him to Buffalo Bill, and he rode the range for Bill as a fence rider for almost two years, he claimed.

Sometime in that period, Parmer blundered into a pair of cattle rustlers who were misbranding calves in a ravine. He told the *Star-Phoenix* reporter in 1932:

> One pulled his Colt 45 and so did I but I jumped the mare at him and knocked him off his horse. He began shooting as he fell but I settled him. Just then I felt a streak of fire through my hip. I was wounded by the other fellow, but I whipped around and got him as he ran.[8]

Then he rode twenty-two kilometres to a doctor who had to lift him off his horse. His boot was full of blood, he recalled, but the two cattle rustlers were in worse shape. They were dead.

After his stint as a fence rider, Parmer became a "faker" at circuses, country fairs, and other expositions and shows, posing as a concrete or "petrified" man. It is thought that he donned a rigid get-up crafted of an inflexible material like plaster of Paris over a lighter inner material. He abandoned that dubious trade when other fakers copied him.

Around 1992, Saskatoon actor, broadcaster, and producer Bruce McInnes happened on Parmer's story and interviewed old-timers who knew him. McInnes was convinced that Parmer had fought in the Civil War with the Quantrill gang and had met the James boys. A reporter who interviewed McInnes wrote:

> Legend has it that Jesse James himself might have visited this area, shortly after a disastrous attempted bank robbery in Northfield, Minn., where several gang members were killed, or captured. The gang fled to Sioux Falls, S.D., where Parmer met them once again, and they all took a trip into Canada. At the time, Jesse had a $25,000 price on his head, dead or alive, and Frank was worth $15,000 in bounty. They only stayed about two months....[9]

McInnes died suddenly in 1998, and with him perished his intriguing television documentary project and the history he had unearthed. One of McInnes's informants was researcher Pat Mallory of the Clay County Department of Historic Sites in Missouri. She has confirmed that the James gang were in the Dakotas. After years of research she has found no evidence that the bandits were in Canada, although she admits it is possible.

Escape to Dundurn

Whether the Parmers were fugitives from American justice or not, Charlie and his son first arrived in the Dundurn area some years before 1905 to have a look around. Earl remembered:

When we got this far Father figured the land was so arid the farmers would never settle it. We would never be crowded, it was just the place he was looking for. But in short order they were plowing all around us. Later, Father said, 'Them farmers will turn this country into a desert.'[10]

They formally immigrated to Canada in 1905 and took up a homestead about six kilometres northeast of the little town, near a little lake, as shown on a map of the rural municipality of Dundurn. The homestead was located at NW 4-34-4 W3, northeast of the Dundurn Army Camp.[11] A map shows the Parmer spread straddling what is now Highway 11. They constructed a sod shack, although some called it a dugout because it was dug about a metre into the ground, located on slightly higher ground where the approach of intruders could be easily spotted.

In the early days most homesteaders took refuge in all sorts of ramshackle structures, even wooden tents, when they first arrived, but as soon as they could they built a better home. Parmer stubbornly clung to his primitive sod shack until the early 1930s, when his son insisted his aged father move into the little wooden house he had built for him. Harvey Mawson's grandfather, Bert Drennan, who homesteaded about twenty kilometres east and south of Parmer's land, described the shack. It was constructed of log and sod. Its thick walls and roof and some rough steps were set into the ground about a metre deep. The steps descended to the shack's only

Parmer in front of his rustic sod shack. – *Photo PH-99-91-4, courtesy of the Saskatoon Public Library Local History Room.*

entrance. Just inside that door was a trap door, under which was a dirt cellar. At night the trap door was left open, so that an intruder bursting in would plunge into the dark abyss below.

For whatever reason, Parmer was skittish, even paranoid, about his personal safety even in the hinterlands of Saskatchewan. Even as an old man in 1932, people say, he still slept with a revolver under his pillow, and always carried it loaded. If enemies were really on his trail, perhaps it was a sensible measure.

Charlie Parmer's son Earl, taken at Dundurn. – *Photo PH-99-91-3, courtesy of the Saskatoon Public Library Local History Room.*

Published accounts mention Parmer's "boys," but Earl is the only son the people of Dundurn remember, though some did recall a daughter who came to visit. Harvey Mawson recounted the visit of Charlie's daughter from the United States. She didn't think much of Parmer's domestic arrangements and promptly returned to her hotel in Saskatoon. Another female relative brought a fine wool suit that he refused to wear, giving it to a neighbour who wore it for years.

Homestead records indicate that the older Parmer was a widower, but if indeed he was ever formally wed, his wife's fate is lost in time. One Dundurn farmer liked to speculate about the origins of Earl, the son. In a list of the women known to have hung out with the James gang, the farmer pointed to the name Mollie Ellsworth, a prostitute. Mollie is said to have "gone east" for a while, which was a coy way of saying a woman had gone away to hide an unwed pregnancy. Glen Peters, also of Dundurn, noticed that Earl's birth coincides with the dates of Mollie's absence. He gleefully speculated that Earl might have actually been Jesse James's son.

Charlie Parmer settled down to a rustic life raising cattle, pigs, and horses. He had a huge Poland China pig that he claimed was "the biggest boar pig in Canady."[12] His thriving herds netted him a hefty sum deposited in a Saskatoon bank. It was rumoured that he also stashed away a cache of $500,000 in American gold coins. No buried treasure was ever found, although bold strangers sometimes still come snooping around the present owner's property with a geiger counter.

Parmer loved his guns, and kept them "cleaned, oiled and loaded." He was such an expert marksman that even after a stroke that left him partly paralyzed, he showed off his shooting skills. Pulling a .38 from under his pillow, he fired several shots, each of which wiped out a day on the calendar.

When in Parmer's extreme old age a hobo invaded the shack and took his prized collection of guns, Earl pursued the thief and got them back. Another gun incident involved the well-known Senator Meilicke, who lived in the area. He was determined to find out if Parmer really carried a gun under his coat. When he thrust a pipe stem against Parmer's back, "first thing he knew only a thin layer of coat material rising abruptly from Charlie's shoulder kept the gun barrel from being rammed up a nostril of his bruised nose."[13]

Among Parmer's confidantes were Daniel and Adi Kohles of Beaver Creek. He promised their little daughter a saddle when she grew up, and he was true to his word.

Another old-timer remembered that a woman he thought was Charlie's sister-in-law, Susan, brought Parmer a gramophone from the United States. But Parmer was too proud to accept such a gift and insisted on paying her. He didn't want her to think he was destitute.

Dundurner Bill Sawchuk recalled how Parmer set up an alarm system for his shack. A bell was attached to a string near the door, and an empty can that would fall and clatter sat on a window sill.

Parmer didn't take kindly to mockery. The Kohles family related to Mawson a story they had been told by Parmer. When a disrespectful youth tweaked his beard several times, Parmer shoved a gun barrel against the young man's chest. The police were called. When the officer arrived, he frisked Parmer, but Parmer had stuck his gun – probably a .38 six-shooter – into his boot, he chuckled later. He suffered no more harassment from the youth.

No Soap and Water for Him

Parmer avoided soap and water as a mustang avoids a harness. Without a woman to ride herd on him, and still living in his "soddy," old Charlie Parmer must have been quite a spectacle. Late in life, Parmer was admitted to a Saskatoon hospital. Alex Sawchuk, who was Charlie's closest neighbour, remembered:

> He was in quite a grubby state. Attendants, while cleaning him up, became alarmed. They thought his skin was peeling. This condition, though alarming, proved to be something altogether different. Charlie had worn his long-johns for so long that body hair had grown through the coarse material. What at first appeared to be flaking skin was actually bits and pieces of deteriorating underwear adhering to his unwashed body.[14]

In his extreme old age, Parmer suffered a stroke. In December 1935, at the age of ninety-six, he was living in the house his son had built for him. Parmer had moved there under protest, complaining it wouldn't be as warm as the soddy with its thick walls of sod, and he was probably right. He died on December 26.[15] Even if he was a grumpy old man, he still had friends who reportedly surrounded him at his death. But perhaps obituaries always say that. At least Alex Sawchuk and Dick James were very attentive to Parmer in his last days, recalled Mawson.

His son was not so lucky. Earl died alone at the age of eighty in July 1950, never having married, leaving no known heirs. He died in a privy, a humiliating and solitary death indeed. Both father and son were buried in the Dundurn cemetery.

Was Charlie Parmer the outlaw of local legend? One could take it on faith that his brief reminiscences in 1932 are truthful. All the rest is conjecture. The legend still thrives in the Dundurn area, and lively written accounts surface from time to time. People in Dundurn have taken the legend seriously enough to establish an exhibit in the Dundurn museum commemorating the infamous old gun-toter.

All that remain in Saskatchewan as testaments to the old man's existence are a grave in Dundurn's Hillcrest Cemetery, Mawson's book, a historical marker,[16] and a couple of photographs and other memorabilia in the museum or in local collections. Still, the legend of Charlie Parmer is an irresistible lure that draws people to the little town museum, and sales of the booklet *Fast Gun* have been brisk enough to pay for gravestones for Charlie and his son.

Only known portrait of Big Tom Hourie. It was to him that Louis Riel surrendered after the Battle of Batoche. – *Photocopy, courtesy Yukon Archives.*

BIG TOM HOURIE
Saskatchewan's Paul Revere

A nineteenth-century Paul Revere galloped across Saskatchewan's plains and parklands carrying vital messages for the government side in 1885 during the Northwest Resistance, commonly known as the Riel Rebellion. Unlike Revere, he evaded capture, but he faced comparable perils. His exploits were legendary: he was a hero on the battlefield and scored a major coup during the resistance. His name pops up in history books like a prairie gopher. Yet nowadays most people have never heard of him.

Thomas Taylor Hourie was born April 30, 1859, at a Hudson's Bay Company (HBC) post in the Touchwood Hills. A post office history claims that Tom's father, Peter Hourie, named Fort Qu'Appelle, where as a HBC employee he had erected a trading post in 1864.[1] Peter Hourie was the eighth child of Orkneyman and HBC employee John Henry Hourie[2] and Margaret, said to be Cree but actually of the Snake (Shoshone) First Nation. Tom Hourie's mother, Sarah Whitford, was also of mixed descent. Her grandfather was an Englishman named Creamer who was associated with the HBC at Moose Factory and elsewhere. Peter and Sarah Hourie had at least fourteen children.[3] Little is known of Tom's life before the resistance.

First Nations chiefs with interpreter Peter Hourie, Tom's father, October 1886. *Front row (l to r)*: Ahtakahkoop, Kahkiwistahaw, Mistawasis. *Back row:* Louis O'soup, Peter Hourie. – *Photo R-B 2837, courtesy of the Saskatchewan Archives Board.*

BIG TOM SWIMS THE SOUTH SASKATCHEWAN

The most remarkable of the legends about Big Tom Hourie is the story of his swim across the ice-choked South Saskatchewan River. Journalists across the country repeated the thrilling story. He was carrying a vital message from General Middleton to Colonel Irvine in Prince Albert during the resistance. As Peter Hourie told it, toward the end of March 1885 as the resistance was simmering, Lieutenant Governor Dewdney sent for his interpreter, Peter Hourie, who promptly headed to Broadview[4] to meet General Middleton. Telegraph lines had been cut, and the general needed Peter's help in finding a courier to travel quickly to Prince Albert with an urgent message for Colonel Irvine.[5] Peter replied that no white man could do it because he would "fall into the mouth of a trap."[6] He proposed that his own son Tom could make the journey.

The general telegraphed Tom Hourie at Humboldt on March 28. Tom wanted to know how much the job would pay, but when the general told him that Peter had ordered him to take the message, Tom dropped the matter of pay, so great was his sense of duty to his father.

At twenty-six, Tom Hourie was a giant, strapping young man towering six foot six (200 cm). That evening he leaped on his horse, after stashing Middleton's dispatch between the inner and outer layers of his vest. From Humboldt he galloped northward all night and all the next day. On the way he encountered Riel's scouts at Hoodoo, about one day's ride from Batoche.[7] Hourie told them he was on his way to Duck Lake because he had heard his brother had been killed there when the Métis thrashed the North West Mounted Police on March 26. Peter Hourie believed that they trusted Tom as a fellow Métis, for they let him pass without further grilling.

As the story goes, Tom reached the South Saskatchewan River at the site of the old Hudson's Bay Crossing just south of Prince Albert on March 30, but there was a glitch – there was no ferry operating. Hourie was stumped. First he tried to pole himself across using a large ice floe as a raft, but he fell into the water and nearly drowned in its mighty current. Somehow he managed to get back to the shore where he had started. With the rashness of youth, Hourie concluded he must swim the frigid waters of the river. He shed his clothes, including the message inside his vest lining, bundled them up, and lashed them onto a miniature raft or V-shaped travois he hastily crafted out of sticks. He hobbled his horse and deposited his saddle in a tree. Gripping a string tied to the travois in his teeth, he plunged into the icy waters, towing the travois as he swam.

Naked, Hourie dodged ice floes and struggled against the treacherous current. "Sometimes the ice would close in on him, and he would get it to part. His whole sides and hips and ribs were all skinned," the elder Hourie recalled. When Tom reached the other side, half frozen, his body was rigid. Shivering, he dressed and staggered to a farmhouse that had just been vacated by terrified settlers. Coals still glowed in the stove. He gathered up some eggs, roasted and ate them. Then he made his way on foot twenty-five kilometres to Prince Albert and delivered the dispatch to Irvine.

Gabriel Dumont didn't believe this frigid adventure really happened, but Dumont wasn't there, and in any case, in his eyes Tom Hourie would have been a traitor to his ancestors. Peter Hourie believed it, and told the story to John Hawkes, author of *The Story of Saskatchewan and Its People*.[8] A newspaper reporter telegraphed an almost identical account to Montreal, where it appeared in the Montreal *Witness*.[9] He told of

> a message brought in by Frank[10] [sic] Hourie, the son of a Government interpreter, and a young man who, by his deeds of daring, has earned for himself a high place in the record of this war. He left Humboldt on the 28th March, with a message from the General to Colonel Irvine. On Monday, the 30th, he reached Clarke's Crossing[11] [sic] when he found that the river had broken up. He tried to swim across amidst the blocks of drifting ice [in the river] and was nearly drowned before he turned back. He tried again at night, however, and was successful.

The accounts raise many questions. First, what was a mixed-descent family doing helping the government side? Government pay cheques were strong bait and could have swayed their loyalties, but more likely it was their cultural links. The Houries spoke English and Cree but not likely French. Their Métis cousins, mixed families mostly of French ancestry in the South Branch area around Batoche, had a list of grievances and were protesting against the government, as Canadian settlers flooded the country in the 1880s. The "English Métis"[12] had many ties with the European, English-speaking community. Although Riel's resistance movement tried to win their support, all the English Métis offered was a promise of neutrality. At first they supported French Métis demands, but Riel's dream of a separate Métis nation alarmed them and the European settlers.

The miraculous new telegraph service was a lifeline to the outside world for remote prairie settlements.[13] Because the telegraph lines had been cut, a courier had to go. But what Peter Hourie asked of his son was not trifling. For starters, he had to evade the Métis living in the Batoche area. Then he had to cross the river, where there were as yet no bridges. (There were ferries in the region, but many of these consisted of a scow pulled along the riverbank by horses or oxen, then released and carried across by the current, the occupants of the scow rowing furiously as they neared the other side.)

Peter Hourie said his son crossed at the old Hudson's Bay crossing. In a Prince Albert radio broadcast in the 1950s, R. Mayson reiterated that Tom Hourie had crossed there, explaining it was near the Fenton ferry.[14] The most direct route was along the Prince Albert-Qu'Appelle Trail from Humboldt, branching northward from the Carlton Trail where Wakaw is now, toward St. Louis.[15] But St. Louis, a Métis settlement, was dangerous for a government scout. The HBC (Fenton) ferry, just west of present-day Birch Hills, was slightly out of his way, but it made sense for Hourie to take that route, veering east to evade the Métis at St. Louis.

Ferries could be used only when the water was clear of ice; in winter travellers trekked across on the ice. Ice break-ups that early were rare,[16] but for a brief interval each spring, crossing was next to impossible by either means because of the spectacular ice breakup. No watercraft could have crossed the South Saskatchewan River in that epic upheaval nature annually staged before the Gardiner Dam was built.[17]

Assuming the ice-break-up did start that early (as it sometimes did), by this time its fury would have subsided, as Peter Hourie's account describes only "drifting ice floes." Even so, the water was icy. The popular belief is that immersion in icy water causes hypothermia and death within minutes, but "polar bear swims" are held in parts of Canada in the winter. People can actually survive up to thirty minutes.[18] The South Saskatchewan River varies in width from 140 metres (460 feet) or less to more than 365 metres (1,200 feet). At that temperature a person could swim 90 metres (300 feet) at most,[19] but Hourie could have found a place where most of the distance could be forded so that the swim was shorter. The fierce current of the mighty Saskatchewan may also have worked to his advantage. If he did swim, and managed to escape the savage undertow, the current could have swept him across in mere minutes.

Big Tom was probably unusually hardy. Tales of the superior endurance of First Nations and Métis peoples crop up in frontier literature. According to one account, "when the water is exceedingly cold, they leap in without a moment's hesitation."[20] Accounts of the Yukon gold rush also refer to the amazing physical prowess of Natives and Métis.

Hourie could have found a scow or canoe on the river's edge and poled or rowed across. Washington crossed the Delaware among the ice floes.[21] Kathleen Rice actually *rode* the ice floes in her canoe one November at freeze-up. But chilling stories of the Yukon, for example, tell of watercraft being crushed among ice floes.

He may have forced his powerful horse to swim across while he clung to its mane. Pioneer Doukhobor Gregori Makaroff, while travelling to Rosthern for supplies, swam his oxen across the river, floating the wagon behind.[22] However, swimming across the ice-strewn river was hazardous even for a horse, and some animals drowned.

Colonel Irvine's Diary

Colonel Irvine's diary[23] recorded that on April 5 there was still firm ice in the middle of the North Saskatchewan River at Prince Albert. Perhaps on March 30 the ice on the South Saskatchewan was still partly locked in and Tom could walk on ice part way and cross a narrow channel of water using a pole or other prop. Author William Butler[24] recorded a heart-stopping crossing of the same river by his exploratory party in November in the 1880s when the ice covered all but a narrow channel in the middle. After trying repeatedly to cross the channel in a watercraft rigged from an upended wagon with oilskin stretched over it, only his

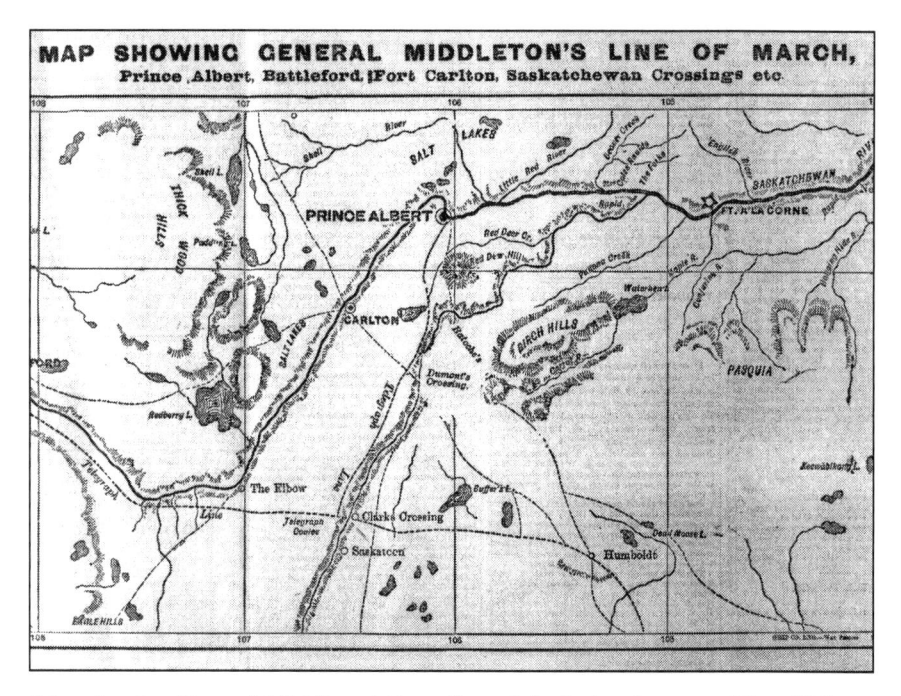

Map showing General Middleton's line of march in Saskatchewan. – *Photo LH 7353 courtesy of Saskatoon Public Library Local History Room.*

Métis companion made it across. In the end he, another man, and a horse walked across that night when the channel froze over.

Was that how Tom crossed – at night? A Montreal reporter hinted that this was indeed the case when he recounted that Tom "tried again at night...and was successful." Middleton, though further south, mentioned "31st March was a bitter cold day...." [25] On April 1, Irvine's diary records, there had been sharp frost the previous night, and the temperature next morning was unseasonably low. Tom didn't reach Prince Albert, twenty-five kilometres away, until March 31. Tom made the journey alone, so only he knew for certain how the crossing was made, and he carried the secret to his grave.

Ironically, there was an alternate route. Messages from the south could be wired to Battleford and then couriered to Prince Albert, and vice versa. On March 30, Irvine's diary records that dispatches were "sent by the commissioner [Irvine] to Regina, urgently demanding support....*Messages have to be sent up to Battleford for transmission* to the East."

On March 31 Irvine's diary records the receipt of two messages that day, one of which was probably brought in by Tom: "Good news came in this afternoon, both by way of Battleford and by a courier from Humboldt, with despatches for Col. Irvine, informing him of General Middleton's presence at Troy [the post office at Qu'Appelle] and his intended movements."

Big Tom delivered more than one message between Middleton and Irvine by that route. On April 1, the diary records, volunteers in Prince Albert were alarmed at the news of the Duck Lake conflict and subsequent fire, and Hourie left with another message. "Despatches [sic] to General Middleton and Lieutenant-Governor Dewdney were sent out by way of Humboldt and Battleford, Hourie taking the former and Poitvin the latter." The scout who set out for Battleford came back the next day as he did not know the way and couldn't find a guide. Hourie knew the way to Humboldt, all too well.

By April 3, there was still snow on the ground, but the roads were slushy. "Hourie returned with despatches, not having been able to cross the South Saskatchewan, as that river has broken up and the ice is running freely." This statement makes the date of his supposed icy dip on March 30 seem questionable, but perhaps he didn't want to tackle it again!

On April 4, Irvine's diary says, water was "still coming up on the river [and the] scout Hourie made a fresh start this morning with the despatches for General Middleton; he has a boat with him to cross the river with." On April 6 Alexander Hourie came in and reported to Irvine that his brother Thomas had "crossed the South Branch with his dispatches [that] morning at Agnew's Crossing, the river there being all clear. Thomas Hourie's horse had been taken away by the half-breeds, and he had to proceed on foot."[26]

On another mission Tom bore a message from General Middleton, then at High Creek, to Col. Irvine, according to his father. Big Tom was staying with a farmer named MacIntosh, who had seen a party of Riel's scouts go by. Fearing their return, the farmer hid Hourie in his house, and Hourie's horse in the barn. Seeing fresh horse tracks, the scouts came back and inquired if MacIntosh had seen anyone. The farmer said no, and the scouts continued on to Fish Creek. Travelling by night,

Hourie passed Riel's scouts. Although they spotted him at one point, he told his father, all three were mired in soft mud. He raced off to Prince Albert on his fine swift horse, dodging bullets from the enemy scouts' rifles, and safely delivered the message to Col. Irvine.

On April 16, Irvine's diary records, "Thomas Hourie, the scout, returned from Humboldt with an autograph despatch from General Middleton, dated the day before yesterday...." On April 19, Irvine and about two hundred Mounties marched out from Prince Albert with Thomas McKay's scouts leading and on their flanks. Perhaps Hourie was among them. Irvine, criticized in the East for inaction, pretended this unauthorized foray was a scouting mission but soon fled back to Prince Albert when it was under threat.

Sometimes Hourie bore bad news. On April 23 he returned from General Middleton's camp at Clarke's Crossing with a letter reporting that Big Bear, with four hundred men, had joined Riel.

OTHER EXPLOITS DURING THE RESISTANCE

Hourie may have been one of the scouts who saved the day for the government side at Fish Creek. They found tracks of Métis horses and raced back to report. When the battle of Fish Creek began early in the morning of April 24, Dumont and his men approached their planned refuge in a coulee, and rode into an ambush. One or two Métis men were killed and the rest fled.[27]

Hourie was also reported to be at the main Fish Creek encounter. Some Métis were trapped in a ravine with no food. Middleton sent Tom Hourie to check out the situation. The Regina *Daily Star* reported it this way:

> Hourie, the interpreter of the force, crept to the edge of the ravine, and shouted to the rebels below: "Is Gabriel Dumont there?"
> "Yes, what do you want with me?"
> "Have you got many men?"
> "Yes, a great many."
> "Will you have a meeting with me? I am Hourie."

When there was no reply, Hourie withdrew.[28]

Both Peter and Tom were in the thick of things during the decisive battle at Batoche in May. Peter said that Tom raced through a blizzard of bullets on Middleton's order, to determine the location of the rifle pits. Another scout had been shot dead on a similar mission, but it was important. By the time the battle started they knew their enemy: "Everything was ready. The ground was known, the enemy's position, the lay of the rifle-pits, their strong and weak points."[29]

Captain French commanded the scouts, and when the government troops advanced to the house of Xavier Letendre (known as Batoche), Tom was right behind French when the captain peered out from an upper storey window and was shot. As French died he gasped: "Well, Tom, I'm shot, but never mind; we were the first that came in here."[30]

Riel Surrenders to the Scouts

After the battle Tom Hourie and two scouts named Armstrong and Diehl brought in Louis Riel, who had fled after the debacle at Batoche. There was a rumoured $1,500 reward for the capture of Riel or Dumont. Hourie was certain which road Riel had taken. Major Boulton and his party headed in one direction, and Hourie and his friends in the opposite direction.

According to most versions of the story, Hourie's group followed a fresh trail starting from Gariepy's (Gardepuis') Crossing and caught up with Riel and five other men on foot. Riel looked small, disreputable, and defeated, but Hourie recognized him. Riding up, Hourie shouted "Hold on, don't fire." Riel's companions knew Hourie, and did not fire. Hourie told him "Mr. Riel, we want you." Riel volunteered to give himself up, and presented a note from General Middleton promising him protection and a fair trial.[31] Wanting the reward, and fearing that Boulton would shoot Riel on sight, they did not reveal Riel's identity when they met Boulton's scouts at one point. "When Tom captured Riel he made Riel get on his horse," Peter said. "Riel still had his revolver, and could have shot them, but he handed it over to Tom who handed it to

Illustration from *Souvenir Number of the Canadian Pictorial and Illustrated War News, 1885*. It was captioned "Capture of Louis Riel by the scouts Armstrong and Howie [sic] May 15th, 1885." – *Image courtesy of Saskatoon Public Library Local History Room.*

Armstrong." As there were not enough horses for all to ride, Hourie and Armstrong slowly led Riel to Middleton's camp at Gariepy's Crossing while Diehl raced ahead to announce Riel's capture.[32]

In Armstrong's version of the story, which he told much later while in his seventies, Riel surrendered to *him*,[33] but by then Tom Hourie was already dead and couldn't contradict him. If Riel knew Tom personally, Riel may have been more willing to surrender to him. Armstrong, on the other hand, went into garrulous detail about the capture. Usually both Armstrong and Hourie (or Howrie, as it is sometimes spelled) are credited with the capture; sometimes Diehl is mentioned too.

In recent decades a fresh look at the Northwest Resistance has recast Riel from rebel outlaw into a Canadian hero. But Tom Hourie's name was stained by the allegation that he was a friend of Riel's executioner. Jack Henderson was a crabby Scottish freighter who had been imprisoned by Riel's forces. When Riel was sentenced to death, Henderson volunteered to be the hangman. Hourie and Henderson may well have known each other.

Next Hourie headed off as General Middleton's guide and interpreter, in search of Big Bear.[34] Middleton and Sam Steele both mention scouts in their accounts of the chase after Big Bear, and Hourie was probably among them.

It is difficult to track Tom Hourie after the resistance ended. The Hourie family was prolific, and there was more than one Tom Hourie in the province. Signing his full name, our Thomas Taylor Hourie applied for scrip money due him as a "halfbreed" and was awarded $240 on August 31, 1885.[35] Homestead records show that he was also issued river lots six and seven in Prince Albert.[36]

HOURIE'S POLITICAL ACTIVISM

While living in Prince Albert, Tom Hourie continued his involvement in public affairs. He appeared midway through a campaign meeting at St. Catherine's School thirteen kilometres west of Prince Albert. His behaviour there shocked Andrew Knox, a onetime member of parliament:

> Just as the program opened in walked Big Tom Hourie 6 ft. 7 in. in height and broad accordingly, [and it was] obvious that he had been imbibing...and wished to establish himself as a cheif [sic] critic of the Conservative Party and policy as well as the conservative Candidate. After some time someone coaxed him out presumably to quench his thirst. Then volunteers were called to mann [sic] the door, but Tom came through without anyone getting hurt. He again took the floor, sometimes he talked politics sometimes he did not and it was soon recognized that it was impossible to carry on the meeting which had to be abandoned. I might say here that I soon discovered that his system of campaigning was considered by a great many people as perfectly all right.[37]

Tom Hourie (left) and others on the move. — *photo by James Peters, courtesy of National Archives of Canada, accession 1958-179, neg C-018940*

NORTH TO THE YUKON GOLD RUSH

Tom Hourie's trail becomes faint until the 1890s when he went to Dawson City, Yukon, with Norman Campbell of Regina.[38] Like thousands of others, they sought gold, which was discovered in the Klondike in 1896. News of the Klondike bonanza reached Canadians ten days before the outside world found out on July 17, 1897, when "treasure ships" arrived in Seattle.[39] There was of course no telegraph or telephone service out of the Yukon. There were no banner headlines at first. The Victoria *Colonist* cautiously mentioned the bonanza as early as July 7, 1897. "Hayes the mail carrier" had just returned from Fortymile and Circle City, site of earlier bonanzas before the richer Klondike gold strikes. He found the two settlements peopled by women and children only, the male population having stampeded to the Klondike, despite bitter temperatures that never reached higher than -47 degrees Celcius and occasionally dropped to -57. "The richness of the new discoveries almost passed belief, single 'pans' returning as high as $800."[40]

A few days later another mail carrier, American A. E. Carr, repeated the news. Despite the blustering headline, "Undreamt of Wealth..."

a skeptical deskman buried the article on page six of the Victoria paper.[41] Apparently, no one paid much attention. After the California and Cariboo gold rushes in 1858 and 1860, newspapers had often bubbled with over-optimistic bulletins of gold strikes that faded into nothing.

When George Carmack registered that first claim on August 17, 1896, the stunning news sent to Ottawa bureaucrats did not spark the commotion that the sight of tons of actual gold did the next summer. The NWMP had a post at Fortymile when news came of the sensational strike. Inspector Constantine alerted the Canadian government and a second unit of constables arrived on June 12, 1897. Canadian government surveyor William Ogilvie also sent the news to Ottawa on January 21, 1897.

With no airplanes or snowmobiles those who couldn't afford the long trip up the Yukon River from the sea by steamboat had to rely on sled dogs, oxen, or horses. The Mounties, who were more experienced at winter travel and northern survival and were not burdened by mining equipment, could mush through the frozen wilderness faster than greenhorns who trekked by the thousands over the Chilkoot and White passes.

In Saskatchewan the departure of local physicians, judges, police chiefs, and businessmen for the Klondike was duly noted in the social columns of the day. Tom Hourie, being of mixed ancestry, did not merit such mention. In the summer of 1897 Saskatchewan and Yukon newspapers declared the need for dogs in the Yukon. Perhaps Hourie was among the Prince Albert group mentioned in September: "A number of dog drivers for the Klondyke mail service left here during the past week."[42] Another news report in August mentioned packs of husky dogs being sent to the Yukon from points east of Winnipeg and some from Moose Jaw. One hundred dogs were expected to arrive in the Yukon.[43]

Big Tom's 1885 exploits were known to the NWMP, so the Mounties might well have invited him along as dog driver, horse minder, or packer. On October 9, 1897 a party of Canadian dignitaries arrived at Skagway with numerous Mounties, dog drivers, and one hundred dogs. Hourie arrived in the Yukon in 1897, and mingled with the first gold-hungry stampeders in the Klondike. It took months to get there, and most didn't arrive until the spring of 1898.[44] The "cheechakos" (greenhorn prospectors) faced fearful risks getting from the coast to the isolated gold fields. The trek from the Gulf of Alaska inland took them over steep mountain passes, canyons, and gorges. Those who went over the Chilkoot Trail had to scale enormous glaciers where snow concealed gaping crevasses into which men and equipment sometimes tumbled. Some men were buried in avalanches; others suffered snow blindness that could be permanent.

Most animals couldn't climb the steep slopes and had to be carried, or take an alternate route. Human packers laboured up the slopes with loads weighing fifty kilograms (one hundred pounds) or more. Later tramways and cable lifts were built over the summit of the Chilkoot Pass. Other people entered by the White Pass, where thousands of horses perished under their heavy loads. Other beasts of burden included oxen and goats, but none were as bizarre as the camels imported to the Cariboo in 1862.[45] Eventually a railway was constructed.

Once over the mountain passes, trekkers still faced great danger. In boats hastily constructed at the foot of the mountain passes, they careened through whirlpools in a deadly canyon, and two sets of rapids, one of which lent its name to the city of Whitehorse.

Still others took one of many river routes, including one through northern Saskatchewan. They faced rapids and raging currents. Huge crashing boulders of ice destroyed their boats or trapped them until spring. On portages they battled snow and ice, swamps and mud. Among the ingenious contraptions designed to carry heavy loads were sleds with square sails for use on ice. One lad and his dogs sailed down the river on his Yukon sled, fashioning floats by tying logs to the sides.

Those who made it to the Klondike faced scurvy, fevers, pneumonia, tuberculosis, spinal meningitis, typhoid from poor sanitary conditions, and even smallpox and malaria. There were forest fires and floods, murders and suicides. Mines caved in. Underground gases exploded when miners lit fires to thaw the permafrost.

Starvation loomed that first winter after the Klondike stampede because the Yukon was cut off in winter from outside sources of supplies. A policeman newly returned to Saskatchewan from the Klondike in July 1897 warned that food must be "taken in overland, because [shipping] companies will carry only 150 lbs. [70 kg] for each passenger up the river."[46] The NWMP decreed that trekkers into the Yukon must carry in 1,150 pounds (520 kg) of food per person, along with mining and camping equipment plus all personal goods necessary for survival.

Newcomers to the region marvelled at the twenty-four-hour daylight in summer. As much as 2800 grams (100 ounces) of gold had been sifted from a single pan, with a thousand dollars per pan typical. But most people had arrived too late; all the best claims were already staked, so they took the first jobs they could find, at ten dollars a day. Saloons did a roaring trade at two to three thousand dollars a day. Prices were astronomical. Sawmills whined continuously to throw together housing and shops for the thousand or so inhabitants, seven or eight hundred of whom had come over the trails that spring. Most were still living in tents.[47] Some even wintered in caves. Not every miner was self-employed. Many toiled for others, especially after large dredging equipment was brought in to mechanize operations.

Peter Hourie may have read in the Regina *Leader* about possible starvation in the Klondike in the coming winter,[48] for in August 1897 he set up a business to turn beef into pemmican for the Yukon, and in September he produced a second batch for the NWMP.[49]

Extreme weather and physical hardship would not have fazed a prairie native like Tom Hourie, nor did they stop the Mounties, although some of them did perish from other causes. Tom's Aboriginal background would have taught him how to brew spruce needle tea or use other natural remedies to prevent scurvy, and he would have been able to hunt and fish for food while city-slickers nearly starved.

Tom's adventures in the Yukon are more obscure than his rebellion activities, but his reputation followed him all the way to the Yukon. The Mounties at Dawson City looked the other way at his transgressions there because of his hero status : "Tom Horey, a half-breed famous as one of the three scouts who had captured Louis Riel...was in town;...the Mounties let him get roaring drunk without arresting him."[50] They may not have known that a man named Thomas Hourie in Saskatchewan had been in trouble with the law for cattle rustling in the 1880s (although perhaps not this Thomas Hourie). Stealing cattle was probably not as serious as horse stealing, which was a badge of honour for young braves undergoing initiation.

How Tom Made His Stake

Despite his early arrival in 1897, Tom Hourie did not hit pay dirt right away, although eventually he made a mineral strike. On January 18, 1907, he filed a placer mining claim for "number fifty-nine above the mouth of the Indian Creek heretofore known as Indian River," having staked his claim on January 14, but was turned down.[51] The reason, written on his application, is now illegible. A Prince Albert MP wrote that Tom "made his stake [in the Yukon] by hunting moose and supplying meat to the miners."[52] During the gold rush he probably lived among other mixed-descent miners and workers, just out of town. His interest in politics spurred him to campaign for safer conditions for miners, to prevent the cave-ins and explosions that sometimes killed ill-fated workers. He served on the Yukon Legislative Association (YLA) in Dawson, and with some labour organizations.

Tom Hourie died of pneumonia in a Dawson City hospital on December 3, 1908.[53] He was listed as a miner by trade. The YLA wired a message of condolence to the elder Houries, who lived at the corner of Albert and Dewdney in Regina. The telegram read in part, "He was a fellow-worker of ours and an honourable man. We have known him intimately during his long residence in this Territory since 1897."[54] He was survived by his parents, a brother and sister at Prince Albert, a sister who was a police matron, and a brother who must have accompanied him on his gold mining trek in the Yukon but had moved to Nevada.

Tom paid a cruel price for his frigid swim in 1885, his father said. "He was healthy and strong like a giant until he swam the river."[55] His father attributed the rheumatism Tom later developed to his 1885 swim, but it must have been made worse by his life in the Yukon. For two years Tom could barely walk, and could not work. "At length he got some better, but it killed him," Peter Hourie said. Tom's mother never got over his death, but Peter proclaimed, "It makes me proud that I had offspring who would obey me to the death."

Figure skater, Norman A. Falkner, skating on a pond or outdoor rink, probably in Ontario where he moved after losing a leg in World War I. – *Photo PH 99-71 from University of Toronto Skating Archives, courtesy of Saskatoon Public Library Local History Room.*

Norman Falkner
One-legged Skating Star

Young Norman glided smoothly around the indoor rink by the riverbank in Saskatoon, perfecting his moves. There was glory in speed skating and hockey, he knew, but it was figure skating that had captured his fancy. He was irresistibly drawn to that rink, mere blocks away from his family's home on Spadina Crescent. Idly he wondered, could a person skate if he only had one leg? He skimmed along on one foot, shifting his weight this way and that to maintain his balance and forward motion. After a few seconds he'd fall, but with each try he managed to glide a little further. You'd still need that other foot to launch yourself, he reasoned. It was a puzzle. But Norman Falkner was blessed with a spirit of independence and a steely resolve. Some day he would figure it out, and amaze everyone.

Stories about disabled people who triumph over their handicaps are always inspiring, but the tale of Norman Falkner is almost beyond belief. This persistent and determined young man did indeed learn to skate on one leg, well enough to perform at ice carnivals throughout North America.

Norman Falkner was born May 29, 1894, one of three sons and one daughter born to Clinton Tully Falkner and his wife Judith.[1] C. T. Falkner had come to the Smithville district[2] just outside the prairie settlement of Saskatoon about 1892. Around 1903, the family moved into

Saskatoon, which officially became a village with a population of 450 on July 1 that year. (It became a city in 1906 with the merging of the three neighbouring communities in what are now Riversdale, Nutana, and downtown Saskatoon.)

The elder Falkner was appointed Saskatoon's city treasurer in 1907. The son of a clergyman, C.T. was active in the St. John's Anglican congregation and was a founding father of the Agricultural Society of Central Saskatchewan,[3] forerunner of the Saskatoon Exhibition.

Norman Falkner learned how to skate as a small boy and played on one of the early hockey teams in the West. But he himself admitted that between the ages of eight and fourteen he was a bit of a klutz at skating. What passed for skates in those days provided little or no ankle support, so his weak ankles would buckle and he'd topple over. Much to his distress, his ineptness barred him at first from playing hockey and from joining the church hockey team.

Then in 1908, when he was fourteen, his scoutmaster saved the day. He scoffed at the idea that Falkner's ankles were weak and prescribed daily exercises, to be increased each day. The youth pursued this exercise regimen, and soon his ankles were strong, sturdy, and unbending. But by that time it was too late for him to be a hockey star – his chums were light-years ahead of him in shooting and scoring.

When his father died suddenly in 1908, a victim of the typhoid epidemics that raged in the city in that first decade of the century due to an impure water supply and poor sanitation, Norman felt he should help support the family. After graduating from public school, on July 2, 1909, he started work as a messenger delivering "advice notices" of freight for the CPR. The job permitted him time off in the afternoons, and he entertained himself by skating at the nearby rink that had just been completed. The rink was likely the Auditorium Roller Rink[4], also known simply as the Skating Rink. It was located not far from the west riverbank, a little south of 20th Street East. The family lived in a house on Spadina Crescent just north of 20th Street East.[5]

With hockey denied him, Falkner took up speed skating. One newspaper clipping claims he was at one time the speed skating champion of western Canada. Falkner and his friend Phil Taylor, another speed skater, raced each other for sheer fun. Phil focused on speed, but Falkner chose to take up "fancy skating" because speed skating races were so rare. He delighted in figure skating, but it "almost made an outcast of me," he wrote. His take on it was not that figure skating was sissy, but that others thought the sport was "for aristocrats, and...a boy who had to work instead of attending school, was no aristocrat."[6] But Falkner stuck with it. He taught himself figure skating by reading books on the subject and became quite expert at it. This probably accounts for his later success at learning to skate minus a leg.

Meanwhile, he continued with his speed skating. In the 1909-1910 season at the carnival Falkner won both the boys' and men's races. In the 1910-1911 season he spent more time practising figure skating, using better skates and a second book of instructions. He learned chiefly by trial and error.

He also performed free skating and barrel jumping, excelling at "turning jumps." At the carnival that year, his rival Phil Taylor won the quarter mile speed skating race, while Falkner won the half mile and one mile races. The seasons from 1912 to 1914 followed much the same pattern. Falkner was concentrating now on figure skating, doing "pairs" with a friend named Edith Findley. They skated singles and pairs for carnivals at neighbouring towns, but Falkner was peeved that they were never invited to perform at their home rink.

In 1914, with the advent of World War 1, young men were enlisting and the ranks of hockey players dwindled in Saskatoon. The local church hockey club invited Falkner to join, but only to "check and back check to keep the opposition off balance."[7] He was not permitted to carry the puck, even though he could skate faster and manoeuvre better than the rest. Still, he played some games with city teams in the provincial league.

For young men, the front was where all the exciting action was, and Falkner was no exception. In April 1916 he enlisted in the army, spending the summer of 1916 training near Brandon, Manitoba. Falkner joined the 96th Battalion, and transferred later to the 21st Battalion. He took his skates to England with him and left them with his grandmother at Watford just outside London, where they remained when he was sent to fight in Europe.

After six months in France, "we had been at the front line (on the outskirts of Vimy) and had just been relieved, when on the way out I was wounded," he wrote.[8] Though the injury to his right leg did not seem severe at first, there were complications, and he ended up having it amputated at mid-thigh.

He was invalided back to England to a hospital near Northampton, where the final operation was performed on his leg. Ordinarily he would have been sent to a place that specialized in amputation cases, but by chance his grandmother had met the wife of the owner of Selby Hall. It was a two-hundred-year-old stone house that was being used for the convalescence of fifty war-injured patients. He arrived there in November 1917 and remained until February 1918. The estate had two lakes, one small enough to freeze fairly solid during the coldest weather.

The skater in him began to eye that lake speculatively, much to the amusement of the staff and his fellow patients. But he sent for his skates. He was determined to continue with the sport despite his handicap. One day he overheard his fellow patients mocking him. In self-defence he began to sketch the possibilities of skating on one leg, the trick he had tried as a youth, albeit by launching his glide with the other leg. (Indeed, throughout the rest of his skating career, he had to be pushed onto the ice.) His reasoning was this:

> Consider a man with only one leg, who finds himself with a good skate on, with nothing to take hold of for many yards in all directions. There is no reason why he should fall forward or backwards, because he has support the length of his foot or the skate, and can adjust the weight over the toe or heel by the slightest ankle control.

But the skater was doomed to fall sideways eventually. Falkner claimed that the remedy was for the skater to bend his knee and then straighten it, thus absorbing the sideways momentum.

> The greater part of this [energy] will be to overcome gravity, but the smaller part, in direct proportion to the amount his centre of

gravity has moved away from the perpendicular and towards the horizontal, will be used for travel in the direction he started to fall. At that point he must turn the skate more or less into that direction. The skate will glide on the ice easily and likely travel in the falling motion and the skate may not yet be on a traveling balance. By repeating the action, however, it can be achieved, and he will be skating.... A thrust with the skate on the ice, followed by a glide on the skate will accomplish this.... The would-be skater persists and modifies the straightening of the knee and the amount he turns the skate in the initial effort and in successive ones, he will travel where he wants to....[9]

Theory is one thing, practice another. Falkner was to take many a tumble before he learned the knack of his improbable new craft. His fellow patients, who nicknamed him "Canada," jeered at the idea. His nurses tried to discourage him. His doctor told him to do anything he wanted but not to hurt the stump. Still, Falkner was determined to conquer his handicap.

Tumbles, but Never Gives Up

Meanwhile, the hockey skates Falkner had asked his grandmother to send had arrived, and the ice on the smaller of the little lakes, really just a pond, froze solid. One morning he put on one of the skates and hobbled out on crutches, alone, to the edge of the pond. He crawled onto the ice and stood up, wobbling a little. Falkner maintained momentum by bending his knee and throwing his body weight from side to side – literally throwing his weight around. He collapsed over and over again, but still he kept on trying. He had a sceptical witness. The eldest of the patients, a Welshman, had come out to see what was happening, and guffawed at Norman's "antics."

The young disabled soldier tried it again the next morning with some degree of progress. Then he defiantly asked the Welshman to invite everyone at the hospital to come out at two o'clock to "watch Canada skate."

Nearly the entire household, other people on the estate, and neighbours who had got wind of the event arrived that afternoon – two hundred of them. In front of the disbelieving crowd, Norman skated, still falling repeatedly. Some of the falls were intentional so he could take a breather. He skated the length and breadth of the entire pond, the size of two hockey rinks.

Then he loaned his skates to some of his bemused witnesses. Novices at skating themselves, they too took many tumbles. The doctor bustled in the next day, examined Falkner for bruises and other injuries, and found none. About six lines appeared in a London newspaper reporting Falkner's remarkable feat.

Norman Falkner, former speed skating champion of western Canada ca. 1920. – *Photo PH 2000-68-1, probably by Herb Elliot, courtesy of Saskatoon Public Library Local History Room.*

Soon afterwards the weather turned mild. The ice melted and with it any chance for more skating in England that season. He travelled from Selby Hall back to Northampton Hospital, and from there to Buxton, where he was fitted with a temporary peg leg until he could get a proper artificial leg in Canada. From Buxton he went to Liverpool and sailed on *Landover Castle* hospital ship for what turned out to be its last trip to Canada. It sank on its return trip to England.

Coping with His Disability

By June 1918 Falkner was sent to Whitby, Ontario. After a series of outings to the "limb factory" in Toronto he was fitted with an artificial leg.[10] While at Whitby, he met a man who would become his lifelong friend, Herb Elliott, a dental technician who loaned him his canoe to paddle out on the bay off Lake Ontario. When the bay froze over in mid-December, Norman ventured out to skate, and Herb accompanied him with a camera. It was he who recorded most of the known still images of Norman Falkner skating on one leg.

Falkner was then transferred to his home military district in Regina, arriving on December 26. On a short leave to visit family in Calgary, Falkner went to a hockey arena to skate. The incredulous manager saw him skating and invited him to perform between periods on New Year's Day. At intermission the manager announced that Falkner would skate one-legged. He had been skating for a full minute without a sound from the audience. Suddenly he fell and did a complete somersault, but recovered and leapt back up in seconds. The audience applauded wildly. His brother later reported that the audience had been speculating on what gimmick he was using. Norman's fall removed any doubts as to the authenticity of the performance. He received fifteen dollars as payment, thus launching his professional career.

Falkner was discharged from the services on January 17, 1919, and he returned to Saskatoon to join his brother Herb in the old family home on Spadina Crescent. While in the city he performed an exhibition in the Greenaway Rink (a structure that briefly replaced the Auditorium Roller Rink, which had burned down,[11] before the better-known Crescent Rink was built on the west bank of the river).

There seemed to be no suitable jobs in Saskatoon for a one-legged man.[12] Falkner did, however, get about twenty-five bookings for his skating act between the last week of January and the end of the season. Off to Winnipeg for six months, he upgraded his schooling under a government programme for returned soldiers. That may have been the extent of his post-elementary education.

After a one-month temporary job in Winnipeg, Falkner headed to Ontario to seek a drafting job. By May 1, 1920, he had found a position with Goodyear, but was laid off six months later. His skating career was gliding along more smoothly. He performed three shows a week from January 15 to the end of March 1920. Norman next accepted a job with the forerunner of Ontario Hydro. They allowed him to honour his skating commitments and to continue doing skating gigs on holiday time. This arrangement was to continue for years.

Falkner on Tour

Falkner obtained bookings in Minneapolis, Duluth, Cleveland, Albany, New York, Boston, Providence, and New Haven in the United States, and in Montreal, St. John, Kingston, Hamilton, London, Windsor, Winnipeg, Regina, Saskatoon, Edmonton, and about a hundred smaller communities in Canada. His biggest tours included one to Vancouver and another to the Maritimes. Sometimes he earned a percentage of the net take; other times he was given a straight fee for skating between periods of hockey games.

In the meantime he had found a woman who didn't mind his missing limb, and married her. In 1929 Norman and his wife, Helen, were invited to join the University Skating Club in Toronto, where he skated regularly until 1963. Around 1941-42, Falkner applied to the Canadian Figure Skating Association to be reinstated as an amateur skater so he could help with judging. It was granted, and then withdrawn. He had to apply to the International Skating Union. Finally, he was reinstated in 1951. Much to his amusement, there was a restriction: he was not to enter any competitions. An amputee in his fifties, he thought, couldn't possibly be much of a threat to competitive skaters!

There are still several members of the Toronto skating club who remember Norman Falkner and witnessed his remarkable talent for skating one-legged. But that wasn't all he accomplished. In a short memorial tribute, his colleague John Booker observed:

> He was one of the world's foremost authorities on golf course ratings and handicaps and playing to an eight handicap. He was also a founding member of the Weston curling club and involved in the building program which got them a rink in 1955.[13]

An Active Ninety-year-old

Falkner moved to British Columbia after his wife's death in 1973. In 1980 he penned his brief memoir, a copy of which was presented in typescript form to the University Skating Club in Toronto, along with the unused right skate of the pair he'd had made in 1935. As a peppy old codger in his nineties, Falkner was still swimming pool lengths every day. In his final year, he was confined to the Peace Arch Hospital in White Rock, British Columbia. Falkner died in 1985 at the age of ninety-two.

Over the years a few press clippings and photographs have surfaced, affirming Falkner's amazing skating career. Only recently his typewritten autobiography was obtained from the University Skating Club archivist in Toronto. In 2000, a short video about Falkner was being produced for the Saskatchewan Communications Network.[14] At the last possible moment a fax arrived from the skating club archivist, announcing she had located some film footage showing Norman Falkner skating one-legged — although he was by then an older man and skating with a female partner — putting to an end any doubts about his extraordinary athletic feats. He was likely, as he claimed, to have been the world's "only one-legged figure skater, ever."

Morris "Two-Gun" Cohen. – *Photo PH 95-68 from* Two-Gun Cohen *by Charles Drage, Courtesy of the Saskatoon Local History Room.*

MORRIS "TWO-GUN" COHEN
A Life of International Adventure and Intrigue

Morris "Two-Gun" Cohen, once a rascal who hung out on Saskatoon's west side, was one of the most flamboyant characters to emerge from the Canadian West. From humble beginnings he rose to become a high-profile figure in England, Canada, the Middle East, and China. His was truly the life of an adventurer and soldier of fortune. In his day, his arrival in a city made headlines, and recently New York author Daniel S. Levy began probing the rollercoaster career of the colourful Cockney. *Two-Gun Cohen: a Biography* [1] was published in 1997, but Cohen is still largely unknown, even in Saskatchewan, where his life veered off in a startling but lasting direction.

Cohen was a paradox. At times he seemed a jovial, fun-loving highroller; at others, a belligerent ruffian. In his early delinquent years he delighted in ripping off trusting victims, but he was also devoted to his family, generous to a fault, and fiercely loyal to his friends. He hung out with low-life characters in bars, brothels, gambling halls, and hotel lobbies, but also mingled with the rich and powerful.

Morris Cohen could have played a mafia thug in the movies, or at the very least, a tough army sergeant or boxer. He looked like a prize-fighter – swarthy and pug-nosed, hefty and beefy, with an aggressive Superman jaw. His 1916 military attestation papers say he was five feet seven inches tall (170 cm), with thick black hair and light brown eyes. Cohen's command of English reflected his trade-school education and boyhood

Cohen with his parents in England. – Photo from collection of Victor D. Cooper, courtesy of Daniel S. Levy.

in London's East End. His speech was peppered with picturesque expressions and lively, street-smart slang, and his voice was gravelly.

Moishe Abraham Cohen was born August 3, 1887[2] and grew up in London, England, in that city's rowdy and tough East End. His parents were Josef Leib Miaczyn and his wife Sheindel, who had escaped to London after fleeing the pogroms in Poland. Morris was named Abraham; he later adopted Morris as his first name, and went by the Jewish nickname Moishe. In addition to Morris, the Cohens had seven other children: Rose, Nathaniel, Leah, Rachel, Benjamin, Sarah, and Leslie.

Daniel Levy compared Cohen as a boy to Dickens's Artful Dodger.[3] En route to school he daily faced racist taunts from Christian boys, and learned to defend himself. Burly nine-year-old Moishe took up street brawling. After flattening one opponent, he was lured into the ring at the People's Arcade, where he began to perfect his boxing skills and earn a few coins to feed his hankering for treats.

His tough Cockney street life shaped young Cohen as a juvenile con artist and petty thief. He started to pull off scams that netted more treat money. When he was twelve Morris was arrested for pickpocketing. He was sentenced to reform school, and in 1901 was transferred to the new Hayes Industrial School. While there he received military training.

In his life story, partly dictated by Cohen and partly penned by his friend Charles Drage,[4] Cohen glossed over his youth as a petty crook and jailbird, omitting legal jams eventually unearthed by Levy. But Cohen's later life seemed to reflect a need to redeem himself and earn respect in the eyes of society, and particularly his family.

IMMIGRATES TO CANADA

Cohen graduated from Hayes in 1905. To separate him from his fellow young hooligans in London, his parents agreed to send him to Canada with a few hundred of the well-known Barnardo children,[5] to earn his keep as a farm labourer. Morris was escorted to Wapella, Saskatchewan, located twenty-four kilometres northwest of Moosomin, to work for a friend of his parents.

Wapella was the one of the first of about a dozen Jewish farm settlements on the Canadian prairies. Between 1881 and 1901 the number of Jewish immigrants to Canada had shot up from 2,443 to 16,401, many of them seeking a haven from persecution in Russia. Between 1886 and 1907, some fifty Jewish families settled on homesteads near Wapella.[6] Among them was young Samuel Bronfman, who was to become the famous Canadian liquor baron during Prohibition.

The family friend didn't really need Cohen, so he was sent to work for Robert Nicholson,[7] a kindly local farmer. While there, the young scallywag learned racier skills than farming – card-sharping – from another hired man named Bobby Clark, a veteran of the Yukon gold rush.

The brawny young Cohen worked hard though, and soon the first farmer demanded that he come back and work for him. Cohen reluctantly went, but he didn't stay long. Soon he lit out for Virden, Manitoba, where he toiled for a few months at a brick factory.

After the fierce winter of 1906-07, Cohen abandoned his job and headed for Moose Jaw. In early July 1907, the Greater Norris & Rowe Circus came to town.[8] Cohen was entranced and asked for a job. The carneys schooled him as a barker to perform in front of a sideshow tent. When the circus left on its prairie circuit, he travelled with it for three weeks, arriving in Winnipeg on July 31. Cohen opted to stay, settling into the Maple Leaf Hotel, which was run by a Russian Jew.

It wasn't long before Cohen was plotting clever swindles again, this time in a scam involving phony gold rings and pocket watches. After his arrest for seducing an underage girl, on April 7, 1909, Cohen was sentenced to six months hard labour and tossed into jail. On his release, he headed for the fledgling city of Saskatoon, where opposite the original

Looking west on 20th Street as streetcar lines are laid around corner of Avenue A (now Idylwyld), ca. 1913. A Chinese café across the street was the site of a robbery that altered Morris Cohen's life. – *Photo LH 4394 by Benjamin P. Skewis, courtesy of the Saskatoon Public Library Local History Room.*

temperance colony on the east side of the river, liquor, gambling, and prostitution flourished on the west side.

Another wave of immigrants was arriving in droves. After the 1900 Boxer Rebellion in China, two thousand Chinese immigrants a year were arriving in Canada, and the infamous head tax was raised to five hundred dollars in 1903.[9] Far from their wives and children, Chinese immigrant men whiled away their leisure hours gambling, along with like-minded Europeans. To the Chinese, fortune in games of chance, as in life, was a goddess to be courted.

The city's early Chinatown district included the 300 block of 2nd Avenue South, the adjoining 19th Street East in the south downtown, and the easterly parts of Riversdale. With Morris Cohen's newly developed skill at cards, he naturally drifted into Chinese gambling houses. That's how he met Mah Sam, whose influence was to alter Cohen's destiny and mould him for his life of international drama and intrigue. The elderly Chinese man ran one such clandestine operation – probably the "gambling den and opium resort" mentioned in a newspaper account of Mah's arrest[10] – behind a reputable business two doors south of the Baldwin Block on 2nd Avenue South. The partitioned-off area is clearly marked on early fire insurance maps of the period.

Mah also had a restaurant, the Alberta Café, at 111 20th Street West. One day as Cohen entered the café, he saw that his friend Mah was being robbed. Cohen floored the armed thief, grabbed the man's ill-gotten booty, and hurled the robber into the street.

The Chinese, who were so often victims of racial bigotry, were dumbfounded that a white man would rescue one of their own people. They welcomed Cohen, a fellow outcast, into their midst, and Mah Sam began to tutor him about the Chinese Nationalist movement and its leader, the much-revered Dr. Sun Yat-sen.

But Cohen did not give up his shady dealings. In August 1910 he picked the pocket of Ire Toder, a Viennese railway labourer, after chatting him up in Wilson's Café at 265 2nd Avenue South. Police officer John James arrested Cohen that same day, and attorney John Duncan Ferguson was hired to defend him. Cohen denied the charge, but after a well-publicized trial, he was sentenced on September 3 to one year's hard labour in the Prince Albert penitentiary.[11]

On September 14 Mah Sam was also nabbed by the police, charged with running a "disorderly house," and sentenced to six months hard labour at the P.A. pen and a hundred dollar fine. He was later transferred to the Moosomin prison. In his biography/autobiography Cohen claimed that the police chief was crooked and Mah was framed. Years later in 1923, after being arrested on an opium possession charge, Mah was released by Judge McLorg, who didn't think the sick old "celestial" would survive another stint in jail.[12]

As Cohen languished in prison in 1911, Dr. Sun was crisscrossing Canada making stirring speeches. He dreamed of freeing China from the corrupt Manchu dynasty, but he didn't covet the Dragon Throne. He defined three basic ideals for the new China: democratic government, a fair economy, and liberation from western imperialism. To reach these goals the country needed a modern communications system, railways, ports, and later on, aviation. These ideas inspired Cohen too, whose family had suffered so much economic and political tyranny.

In September 1911 Cohen was released, and he hightailed it back to Saskatoon. He looked up Mah, who continued to thrill him with dreams of revolution in China. The next month, on October 9, an ill-timed bombing led to an uprising that threw China into revolution. Dr. Sun, then in Denver, rushed back to China. In early December 1911 a provisional republic was set up with Dr. Sun as president. In February 1912 Sun offered the presidency to a powerful warlord, General Yuan, to gain his military support.

Chinese immigrants in Canada were elated by the political shake-up in their homeland. In 1912 Morris Cohen travelled with Mah to Calgary, where Cohen was inducted into the Tongmenghui, a secret society which preceded the Kuomintang (KMT, later pronounced Guomindang). In Calgary he met Bert Finch, who persuaded him to move to Edmonton to join his business, the National Land Co.

Though often in legal hot water because of his taste for gambling, Cohen still networked in respectable circles. Newsmen and politicians often exploited his links with the Chinese community, and Cohen pulled strings among powerful pals to help Chinese friends in trouble. In April 1913 he was appointed a commissioner of oaths in Edmonton, where he helped his Asian friends get landed-immigrant status.

By 1914 the real estate boom was tottering, and he was in trouble again – a shady real-estate deal involving a club charter in Edmonton, a police raid on a gambling den, and a crackdown on gambling and prostitution. Houdini-like, he wiggled out of these scrapes and stayed out of jail.

In June 1914 World War I broke out, and Cohen enlisted with the 218th Overseas Battalion, also known as the Edmonton Irish Guards and famed for its ethnic mix. He was soon appointed acting sergeant, and he and his unit joined twenty thousand men in Sarcee City just outside Calgary.

In January 1917 Cohen's battalion became a railway construction unit. They shipped out of Calgary in February and sailed to England. Soon the 218th melded with the 211th to become the 8th Battalion, Canadian Railway Troops. In London Cohen slipped off to make whoopee with a prostitute.[13] Later, a bout of gonorrhea prevented Cohen from leaving

Sergeants of the 218th Battalion in 1916. Morris Cohen is seated third from left.
– *Photo courtesy of the Edmonton City Archives.*

with his battalion on April 17. Cohen was punished for his sins by a demotion to sapper (a soldier in an engineering corps responsible for digging trenches and building other defences). Cohen rejoined his comrades near Ypres in Belgium on September 8, just after the Battle of Paaschendaele began.

In China, the 1911 revolution that ended centuries of stability – however dictatorial – had only brought chaos. Coming decades were marked by famine, floods, disease, banditry, and corruption, and the brutality and upheaval of a warring feudal society. When Yuan outlawed the KMT as part of his plan to ascend the Dragon Throne himself, Dr. Sun fled into exile in Japan. Far from being unified as Sun had dreamed, China was controlled by battling warlords, each defending his own turf. On June 16, 1916, Yuan died and was replaced by a new leader under a semi-republican government. In 1917, at the age of eleven, the deposed child emperor Pu-Yi (now spelled Puyi) was re-crowned emperor for twelve days and was immediately deposed again. In August Dr. Sun returned to Canton, but his attempt to set up a government failed, and he fled back to Japan.

During World War 1, 190,000 Chinese laboured for Britain and France in Europe, the Middle East, and elsewhere. Cohen was again put in charge of a unit of Chinese railway workers building temporary railway lines to move troops and equipment. They were unschooled peasants, not the businessmen he was used to, but Cohen said he understood them well enough to get them to work effectively.

In February 1918 Cohen suddenly couldn't move his jaw. The problem was diagnosed as arthritis of the right articulation of the jaw, possibly caused by gonorrhea. Although Cohen was in pain, he continued his work, and when the Germans advanced in March 1918, he and his unit destroyed the rails behind the retreating troops so that the Germans couldn't use them. But by June the pain became too severe, and Cohen was sent to a hospital in Southampton, England. There the doctors wired his mouth shut, a severe ordeal for an irrepressible raconteur. By October 25 he was out of hospital and off to a base at Seaford.

When peace came on November 11, 1918, Cohen could not contain his joy when a nurse told him the war was over. He left the hospital and went AWOL. He went AWOL twice more before being shipped home to Canada with his battalion. Back in Edmonton, he was discharged from the army as medically unfit in March 1919. He then opened a real estate office and invested his money in mining.

By now, Morris Cohen was starting to yearn for respectability. He joined the Great War Veterans Association (GWVA) and threw himself into a campaign for government benefits to help ex-soldiers fit back into civilian life.

Shortly afterward, in May 1919, Dr. Sun's followers formed the Keng Wah Aviation School on the outskirts of Saskatoon to train Chinese pilots for his Nationalist cause.[14] Cohen donated money towards the fifty thousand dollars raised by the Chinese for this project.

Meanwhile the political pot was bubbling in eastern Europe. The Bolsheviks had just overthrown the last Russian czar in 1917 and seized power in Russia, and the country was rocked by civil war. Communist ideas were spreading to China, and in 1921 the Chinese Communist Party was established. Reds soon joined the Kuomintang, whose guiding principles included ideas compatible with socialism. Yet there were also right-wing elements. Sparks of dissent began to kindle within the KMT.

Political control in southern China was still unsteady, and for years Sun jousted with the warlords for power, fleeing to exile more than once. After being elected provisional president of the southern republic he was again driven out in 1922, and returned in 1923.

While foreign powers gambled on new ideologies, Morris Cohen continued to gamble in illegal card games. He kept his hand in at the GWVA and in local politics, and he continued to protect the harassed Chinese, who even lost the right to vote federally in 1921.

Sun had heard about Cohen's defence of Chinese-Canadians, and he contacted Cohen about finding a Canadian company to build a vital railway link from Canton to Hankow. Cohen went to Vancouver, where he tracked down a new railway construction firm that agreed to build the railway. Cohen was to go to China and wait for the arrival of Cummins, the company vice-president.

COHEN IN CHINA

Cohen sailed from Vancouver on November 23, 1922, and arrived December 12. He soon wangled an interview with Dr. Sun's secretary. That day he also met Sun's wife, Soong Qing-ling, and thus began a lifelong friendship. He was quite smitten with the dazzling Mme. Sun. She was pretty and charming, and Cohen had an eye for pretty women. Mme. Sun came from the prosperous, western-educated Soong family. The Soong sisters were divided by their marriages. Her sister Soong Mei-ling married Chiang Kai-shek.[15] Mme. Sun's support of her husband's "People's Livelihood" doctrine threw her into the camp of radicals that craved social change, while Chiang's KMT leaned to the right and maintenance of the current system.

Soon Cummins arrived in China, and the railway contract was signed. Cohen talked his way onto Sun's payroll as a bodyguard, with the title of adjutant. As a former boxer, he passed on his fighting skills to the two hundred or so bodyguards who made up Sun's "army."

Dr. Sun took over the military government and reorganized the KMT and the army in 1923, while Chiang ran the new academy for soldier training. The warlord era peaked in 1924, and the communist-KMT coalition controlled southern China from 1924 to 1927. Communists in the KMT meanwhile were plotting a peasant revolution.

Although in the Drage biography Cohen skirted around his early scuffles with the law, his storytelling gifts emerged when he told about his adventures in China. Author Daniel Levy doubts the truth of many of Cohen's tales, in which he usually cast himself as a hero. In the 1920s, he said, he helped to wipe out the Bias Bay pirates who terrorized Chinese and Europeans alike on the waterways around Canton. The pirates, dressed as passengers, would board boats, and once at sea, hijack and loot them, sometimes taking wealthy passengers hostage. Cohen claimed he helped a local warlord get guns and boats for the capture of seventy-five pirates, who were executed for their sins. But the pirate problem didn't go away.

It was while in the service of Dr. Sun that "Two-Gun" Cohen acquired his vivid Old West moniker. In an Oriental shoot-out, he was nicked in the left arm. The near-calamity frightened him so much, he then practiced shooting with both hands, and thereafter always carried two guns. By 1923 he and a fellow bodyguard dubbed themselves generals. Later he received the official title of honorary general, although he never officially commanded an army.

Morris Cohen never really learned Cantonese, or Mandarin either. However, after centuries of British imperialism, many Chinese in the population-crammed areas spoke English, including Dr. Sun and his wife. The houseboys could not get their tongues around Morris's name, so they called him Mah-Kun. When speaking to poorly educated Chinese, Cohen spoke a curious brand of pidgin English. He mimicked their own speech patterns in English, as in: "Pirates pinch'um John Lake wallah-wallah; governor wanting you bring back chop chop."[16]

As Sun's bodyguard, Cohen sometimes stood in the line of fire, as his master's life was often in peril. He told of a time when he foiled four armed hit men who ambushed a train in which Sun was riding. Spotting the would-be assassins, he shielded Sun with his body and then "let fly" with a barrage of bullets. The hit men fled. At least that was his story.

Morris Cohen with Chiang Kai-shek. – *Photo from collection of Victor D. Cooper, courtesy of Daniel S. Levy.*

On March 12, 1925, Dr. Sun Yat-sen died of cancer. His last words were: "Peace...struggle...save China."[17] Cohen felt lost, in despair.

The following year, Chiang made the historic Northern Expedition to unify China that Sun had longed to do. Chiang's right-wing KMT then staged a coup d'état, severing itself from the communist faction. On August 1, 1927, the communists led an armed uprising that launched a titanic struggle between left and right for control in China. It was to last until 1949, except for a brief "marriage of convenience" during the Sino-Japanese War. The land-hungry Japanese began their long assault on China in September 1931, starting with Manchuria in the northeast.

Following Sun's death, Cohen worked in southern China for various leaders and military men who claimed to be aligned with Chiang's KMT. Chiang had been a disciple, so to speak, of Dr. Sun, but over time had become corrupt and ruthless. Although he was a harsh dictator, he was still the choice of Western nations because of his right-wing stance, rejection of communism, and eagerness to keep things the way they were.

Some warlords opposed Chiang's plan to unite China, and they wanted weapons. Having already helped Sun Yat-sen obtain arms, Cohen naturally turned to profitable gun-running, or as he put it, buying and selling "sewing machines." With southern China perpetually in conflict, arms dealers flocked to China and Hong Kong. Cohen's extensive contacts with Chinese business and political moguls made it easy for him to act as a go-between. He arranged to buy gunboats, machine guns, aircraft, anti-aircraft artillery, explosives, ammunition, and thousands of rifles from European countries, charging 5 per cent for his services.

His post-Sun adventures, Cohen said, included outwitting a bomber on a Canton wharf and leading troops into battle against the Yunnanese (the closest he probably came to being a real general). He claimed to have averted a run on the Cantonese currency at the central bank. Another time he was sent to deal with a reeking package that he thought was proof of chemical warfare. He transferred the parcel to the proper authorities.[18]

Chiang feared the communists more than he did the Japanese. On December 10, 1930, he launched the first of a series of "Red Bandit Suppression" or "Extermination" campaigns against them. Taxation, already crippling, was increased by the KMT to pay for arms. To make matters worse, drought and famine struck the calamity-ridden country, and bandits harassed the rural areas.

In the conflict the Reds took weapons as spoils of war from the KMT, who had obtained them with the help of foreign powers. The communists relocated to new headquarters at Yenan in Shansi (now Yan'an in Shaanxi) province in the so-called North-West after the arduous and tragic Long March begun in October 1934, led by Mao Tse-tung (now called Zedong). Of the original one hundred thousand members, more than ninety thousand perished.

In the thirties, many Chinese, especially rebellious students, were furious at Chiang Kai-shek for not taking a stand against the Japanese swarming unbidden into their country. In December 1936 there were noisy protests in forty cities. Chiang went to Sian (Xi'an) near the communist base in Shansi to plan a final bandit extermination campaign. In a surprise move on December 12, 1936, Chiang was kidnapped by Chang Hseuh-liang (now Zhang Xueliang), the Manchurian leader known as the Young Marshall. Chang was one of Chiang's allies, yet he believed that instead of fighting each other, the nationalists and communists should combine their forces against their real foe, the Japanese. Chiang grudgingly accepted his conditions (the most important was to fight the Japanese invaders) and supposedly agreed to end the anti-communist campaigns. Thus began the Sino-Japanese War, a conflict that was to last from 1937 until the end of World War II in 1945.

No lifetime of adventure would be complete without a stint as a spy. During the war Morris Cohen served as a minor agent for Britain's Special Operations Executive (SOE), a sabotage and propaganda body formed in 1940. Their Far Eastern headquarters were in Singapore. According to Levy, Cohen was a friend of fellow Canadian Francis Kendall, a secret service man with the SOE who commanded "Force Z."[19] Not surprisingly, little is known about Cohen's work as a secret agent, except that Kendall paid Cohen to report on goings-on.

On Christmas Day 1941 the Japanese overran Hong Kong. At midnight on Boxing Day, several armed Japanese soldiers stomped into the lounge of the Hong Kong Hotel and seized Morris Cohen. He was taken to an office building, questioned, released, and then seized again. On January 5, 1942, he was herded onto a parade ground with other civilians from Japan's enemy countries. Most of the colony's British, American, European, and Dutch civilians were then interned in filthy and crowded rooming houses, without regard to gender. Cohen was first confined in a hotel-cum-brothel in a small room with a British woman and child. Soon the civilian prisoners were corralled in one camp on Stanley Peninsula. Cohen was among them. That month the military prisoners were segregated by nationality into different camps. Fifteen hundred Canadians and some British navy personnel were sent to North Point camp on the island. Most British prisoners were sent to Shamshuipo, and the East Indians to Mau Tau Chung on the mainland.

Cohen was relieved to learn he was regarded as a civilian and not a Chinese officer as his title implied. The *Kempetai*, the Japanese secret police, took him to a private prison in Kowloon, where he was kept in a tiny office for two nights. Next he was moved to a basement cell bare of furniture and left to stew about his fate. When his captors came to question him, boasting about what their spies had found out about him, most of which was "hooey," he said he didn't know what they were talking about. Enraged, two men kicked him repeatedly. When one of them attacked him with a bamboo stick, Cohen lost his cool and clobbered the man. For that he received a severe beating and was dragged back to his cell to shiver all night.

Later when he piously told his captors he was now retired and spending his time fund-raising for the sick and wounded, they beat him again. (He did do charitable work, but they might not have approved – he collected funds to aid refugees and buy medical provisions for soldiers.)

One day at Stanley, four Chinese in a crowded cell next door tried to escape, and their cell-mates were dragged out and beaten. Two were killed in the violence; the other two were beheaded later.[20] Another day he heard a rumour that *he* was to be beheaded. After giving away a secret cache of money he had sewn inside a coat lining, he was taken to the interrogation room and told to kneel as a Japanese swung his samurai sword high over Cohen's neck. Over the thundering of his heart he heard the sword come slashing down, but his head remained attached. (This tactic was often used to terrify captives.) After a barrage of kicks it took Cohen, no longer a young man, two weeks to heal. But after his dance with death Cohen felt sheer bliss at merely having survived.

Chosen to house families with children, Stanley appears to have been a little more humane than other Hong Kong POW camps. After the wreckage left by looters was cleaned up, the sunny location swept by sea breezes made it a healthier place than most, at least until 1942, when food shortages led to near starvation and diseases of malnutrition.

As a civilian, Cohen was not horribly tortured as described in newspaper reports, wartime diaries, and postwar accounts by prisoners in Japanese POW camps. The Japanese probably did not know that he had been a spy. Luckily he was not held captive until the end of the war like most POWs.

But Cohen loved his chow, and food shortages must have been almost unbearable to him. Internees who knew him at Stanley reported that Cohen radiated good cheer, a perpetual sunbeam despite the near-starvation diet, diseases, and misery of camp life. Cohen later thought his Jewish background had saved his life, that centuries of abuse of the Jews had prepared him for hardship.

Cohen was not alone among interned Jews. An estimated fifteen thousand Jewish refugees from central Europe were imprisoned in the Shanghai area alone. When the Japanese surrendered, some six thousand gaunt Jews were found alive in seven camps in that area.[21]

At the outset, Cohen's fleshy padding protected him somewhat against starvation, but like the others he shrank in bulk during his ordeal. Still, he seems to have fared relatively well for a man of his age. The five hundred dollars inside his coat lining and his skill at bartering for food from the black market for himself and his cell-mates helped assure his survival. A friend on the outside brought him care packages, at great risk to herself. The courage and generosity of the Chinese, East Indians, and other nationals who were not interned because the Japanese wanted their co-operation is praised in many books. Even Cohen's Japanese banker friend, after trying to bribe him to collaborate, advised him to keep a low profile, and brought food and small luxuries like cigarettes and liquor and news from outside.

Internees in most Japanese camps in Hong Kong and slave-labour camps in Japan were not so lucky. Red Cross parcels from home were hoarded by the Japanese and few were given to the internees. (Toward the end of the war the Japanese themselves were beset by severe food shortages, as were the Chinese.) Camp inmates suffered from diseases of malnutrition – beriberi, rickets, and pellagra – and related conditions – paralysis, blindness, and "electric feet," an intensely painful condition resulting from nerve damage. There were other plagues: dysentery, malaria in some places, diphtheria, typhus, infected sores, and swarms of insects. In many Japanese camps medical care and medicines were scant, or actually withheld from the internees. However, there was a hospital at Stanley.

A Defence Department report in September 1945 said that 1,689 prisoners had been captured by the Japanese at Hong Kong out of 1,985 Canadians stationed there. Canadians released from those POW camps included several from Saskatchewan.[22]

BAAG, the British Army Aid Group that included some SOE members who had evaded capture, was formed to help POWs escape. A secret network linked key people in Hong Kong prison camps with aid agencies, but most prisoners in the civilian camp at Stanley stayed out of it because of official plans for a prisoner exchange. Had Cohen been involved in this cloak-and-dagger activity he might have suffered the fate of several men who were beheaded as punishment for their underground activities. Still, he must have heard the news that came in on two wireless sets hidden in the camp.

One day the Stanley internees heard that some American prisoners were to be sent home in exchange for Japanese prisoners. That group departed on June 29, 1942. Those left behind enviously watched the ship of freedom depart, and struggled on. But in February 1943 rumours of a second prisoner exchange were confirmed; Canadian internees and others with families in Canada would depart soon. Morris Cohen took advantage of his Canadian status to get on that list.

Most internees would not be released until September 1945, and many others did not survive. Author Dave McIntosh reported that from 1942 to 1945, 133 Canadian soldiers died in North Point and Shamshuipo POW camps, including 4 who were executed. Another 136 died in camps in Japan, some by torture. Nor were civilians immune to abuse. The Japanese reportedly killed some Canadian civilian internees; others died while in captivity. Overall figures for *all* POWs and internees from different countries are even more shocking: about 27,000 prisoners died in one camp that housed about 50,000 – 500 deaths per day.[23]

Cohen left Hong Kong on September 23, 1943, on board a Japanese ship. He had shed eighty pounds (over thirty-five kilograms) while in the camp. The prisoner exchange took place at an Indian seaport, as fifteen hundred former prisoners and seventeen patients on stretchers sailed to America by way of South Africa and South America. In New York the Canadian passengers were loaded onto a train to Montreal, where they were debriefed by Canadian security officials. Because he had served as an SOE agent for the British in Hong Kong and China, Cohen was ordered to keep mum about his work for them as he might endanger other prisoners. This accounts for his silence about his spying activities when he told his life story to his friend Charles Drage.

According to Levy, Cohen tried to market his special Chinese networks and knowledge to Allied intelligence services, to no avail. He was given $6,118.75 in back pay and dismissed. The FBI wouldn't even let him into the United States – his unsavoury past had caught up with him.

After shining like the moon in the reflected glory of Dr. Sun, the loss of face must have been crushing to Cohen. Still, he was fêted by Jewish society in Montreal at a dinner where he was welcomed by Samuel Bronfman, the former Wapella resident who was then head of the Canadian Jewish Congress.[24]

The communist takeover in China after the 1949 revolution left him wriggling in discomfort – he had sided with the forces of the right for so long. Cohen visited his old haunts in China, and although he now claimed to support the new communist regime, he could not find a place there and sadly decided to return to Canada, only to discover he was not needed here either.

The Drage biography hints at Cohen's relationships with women. Mme. Sun frowned on his monthly visits to Hong Kong brothels. She tried matchmaking for him, but it was no use. Asked why he didn't marry some nice Chinese girl, he replied: "A good Chinese girl would never marry a foreigner and a bad Chinese girl I don't want!"[25]

Marriage was a last unexplored frontier for him, so Cohen took advantage of his celebrity status to woo an attractive younger wife. On June 18, 1944, in Montreal he married thirty-eight-year-old socialite Judith Clark, who was swept away by "General" Cohen's swashbuckling past. They spent their honeymoon in Banff and Lake Louise. Their marriage was warm and loving at first. With his lavish habits, Cohen seemed kind and generous. The couple enjoyed the Montreal social whirl, and he loved to entertain eminent Chinese guests at local Asian restaurants. He adored kids (although the couple, perhaps wisely, had none).

His adventures as a gun-runner, go-between, and international fixer were not hot credentials in the job market. Without anything meaningful to do, he often roamed to China, England, Israel, and other distant

Cohen being interviewed on CBC program, *Front Page Challenge.*
– *Courtesy CBC Archives.*

locales, leaving his wife alone to manage the prosperous fashion business that supported them. A plan to establish a movie studio fizzled. A fledgling import business failed. Cohen occupied himself with reciting his memoirs to his friends. His friend Charles Drage wrote it all down, adding his own observations to link Cohen's patchwork of memories.

Judith tried to prop up their failing marriage, but adventurers aren't usually good husband material. After their divorce became final in 1956, Cohen slunk back to England, where he was a hero to his family at least. He lived there until the end of his life.

Extraordinary and far-fetched claims float around on the internet about Cohen's role in Chinese history. An article in the *Jerusalem Post* in

2000 stated that Cohen helped to establish relations between China and Israel.[26] Another website stated that he was a "spymaster" in China, "a legend in the annals of espionage," "nerveless, intrepid and daring."[27] This imaginative and quite false account states that Sun obtained funds from a secret society in Japan, in return for control of the opium trade in China. The article claimed Cohen interrogated, tortured, and even executed "conspirators" exposed by his "vast network of spies."

Still another source[28] said Cohen's life story inspired Gary Cooper's dashing character in the 1936 movie *The General Died at Dawn,* based on a novel by John O'Hara. The movie does contain a train ambush, similar to Cohen's account of saving Sun from hit men. O'Hara may have known about Cohen, but historical novels are usually a complex alloy of fact and fiction. The character Jones in Frank Capra's 1933 film *The Bitter Tea of General Yen* resembles Cohen more than Gary Cooper's character does. Although the author of the book on which the film was based lived in Canton when Cohen did, it is impossible to confirm that the story was inspired by Cohen.

A recent documentary entitled *Two-Gun Cohen*[29] is more accurate. It includes a clip showing Cohen as a portly and jovial old man on *Front Page Challenge.* Pierre Berton said to him, "I keep reading reports that you are dead, that you have been killed.... How do you survive?" Cohen gleefully quoted Mark Twain, saying that the reports of his death were greatly exaggerated.

When asked in 1943 why he had repeatedly risked his life in China, he responded, "Because I love those people."[30] One reviewer called him "Cohen of China," likening him to Lawrence of Arabia.[31]

Jean Ewen, 1931. – *Photo PH 98-111 (detail) from private collection of Tom Kozar, courtesy of Saskatoon Public Library Local History Room.*

JEAN EWEN
China Heroine

Saskatchewan's Jean Ewen was arguably one of the most intrepid Canadian women of her time. In the 1930s the young Canadian nurse tended sick peasants and injured warriors, delivered babies, trained nurses and peasant paramedics, and taught methods of sanitation in faraway China. In the chaos that followed she would meet major figures on the world stage, and her name would appear in history books.

Jean Ewen was born in Scotland on December 24, 1911, the daughter of revolutionary blacksmith Tom Ewen (later known as Tom McEwen), who helped forge her own feisty spirit.

Jean was the eldest of four; her siblings were Bruce, Jim, and Isobel. She spent part of her childhood at the prosperous Wilson farm at Harris, Saskatchewan. Jean didn't go to school until she was ten. This lack of early formal schooling, common in isolated rural Saskatchewan in the early twentieth century, helped to form independent citizens who had not passed through the blender of conformity.

At the ranch Tom McEwen was introduced to socialist ideas by the rancher's wife, who had studied at the Rand School of Socialism in New York. He soon found Fabian socialists at the ranch too bland and in about 1923 moved his family to Saskatoon, where he joined a group that later became part of the Communist Party. Jean later suggested rather bitterly that her father was more interested in being father to a revolution in Canada than in parenting his own brood. As he spent most of his time working for the cause, his children were forced to rely on themselves.

Like many other prairie women, Jean's mother, the former Isobel Taylor, nursed victims of the Spanish flu of 1918. Both Jean's and her father's autobiographies say that Isobel died of that flu, but Jean's brother Bruce insisted that his mother died in the early twenties, and he had the death certificate to prove it. Weakened by the flu, Isobel was sent to a hospital where she contracted tuberculosis, and it was that deadly disease that finally killed her, he said.[1] Or perhaps it was despair. According to her granddaughter Laura Meyer, the hospital where Isobel lived her final years was a mental institution in Weyburn. Isobel became depressed after nursing flu patients in 1918, and modern medicines and therapies for treating depression had not been discovered. Jean was only about ten when her mother died in Weyburn, far from her family. In later life Jean "had an aversion to the notion of being discarded,"[2] which probably began with the early death of her ailing mother – Tom apparently never visited his wife.[3] Not a single photograph of Isobel remains.

So the family was motherless while they lived in Saskatoon. City directories show that "Thos. A. Ewan" successively lived in two houses in the prairie city. In 1923 the family was living in a tiny house at 424 Avenue I North. By 1924 they had graduated to a grander residence at 807 Avenue K North, for years the only dwelling on the block. Laura Meyer remembers an older-style stucco house on Avenue K, but the large, roomy house at that address is now sheathed in cedar.

After Isobel's death, the Ewens had a housekeeper named Laura Johnson, an American with flaming red hair. Jean named her daughter after Johnson. In Saskatoon Jean attended Westmount School and Bedford Road Collegiate. In 1926 she might have rubbed shoulders with Ethel Catherwood, the famous Olympic athlete, or Ken Peaker, well-known Saskatchewan musician. Jean's father worked as a blacksmith on the city's west side[4] and became a prominent union organizer.[5] His movements were tracked by RCMP spies.[6] Tom's firebrand activism soon catapulted him into the upper ranks of the Communist Party of Canada.

Growing up, Jean battled fiercely with her prickly, strong-willed father, and in this stormy cauldron she grew tough and determined to make her own way in those desperate Depression years. Her autobiography, *China Nurse 1932-1939: A Young Canadian Witnesses History*, describes her upbringing in Canada and her nursing career in the thirties.

In about 1927 the party summoned Tom to Winnipeg, and he uprooted his family again. Meyer recalled her mother's strength of character in her relationship with strong-willed Tom. When Jean announced her plan to become a nurse, her father scoffed, "You'll never be able to do it." Her retort prefigured Trudeau's famous "Just watch me."[7] In Winnipeg, although not a Catholic, Jean attended the Catholic-funded St. Joseph's School of Nursing and graduated in 1931. When she had almost finished her second year of nursing school, her family moved to Toronto.

Tom's four children all shared a passionate sense of social responsibility. They were "always striving for recognition from the only parent they knew," Laura mused. The younger Isobel worked tirelessly for the Party, and the two brothers, Bruce and Jim, both served in Canada's Mackenzie-Papineau Battalion in the International Brigades, opposing Generalissimo Franco's fascist forces in the Spanish Civil War, a cause old Tom would have embraced. Jean was to embark on an equally bold but thoroughly independent course that should have pleased her father, yet he scarcely mentioned her in his autobiography[8] which applauds only his second daughter, Isobel, who was evidently more pliable.

Tom Ewen used the pen name McEwen. He was variously known to the RCMP as Ewen, Ewan, and McEwen. Some say the name McEwen was bestowed upon him by an arrogant RCMP bureaucrat on realizing Tom was Scottish.

When Jean graduated as a nurse, Canada was sinking into economic depression and Saskatchewan was mantled in dust. Jobs were scarce. Jean's friend Agnes spotted an ad for nurses to serve with the China mission of the Franciscan Fathers of the Sacred Heart Province. In China many hospitals were run by western churches, and that's where the nursing jobs were. Signing on with the Franciscan Fathers might have been comparable to joining a modern aid organization like Doctors Without Borders. Ewen and her friends Agnes and Rose were gung-ho to go. At St. Joseph's Hospital, a symbolic perpetual flame was lit for the

Ewen and friend, upon graduation from St. Joseph's School of Nursing, 1931. – *Photo PH 98-III courtesy of Saskatoon Public Library Local History Room.*

three plucky young women in recognition of their courage. It was not snuffed out until their return.

Matters were not going so well on the home front for Jean's family. In the 1930s many of the dispossessed, especially in the prairies, looked to various forms of socialism to ease their economic miseries, while the chieftains of industry and politics looked on in horror. Bolshephobia, the Red Scare, had been taking hold in Canada. In December 1931, Canadian newspaper headlines blared the news that eight communists had been arrested and charged with sedition. Among them was her father. Soon another headline announced that the Communist Eight had been sentenced to five years in Kingston penitentiary.

Just as an appeal was launched on their behalf, Jean arrived in Toronto to say goodbye to her family, but she couldn't bear to go to court and witness her father's disgrace. The guilty verdict was not altered. She worried about her younger siblings, especially Bruce and Isobel, but they managed to find modest after-school jobs to sustain themselves.

And so, in March 1933, as the cell doors clanged shut on her father in Kingston Pen, Jean and her colleagues headed west to Vancouver, where they boarded the *White Empress* bound for the Orient. After stopping in Hawaii, where the young "missionaries" cavorted with sailors till dawn, they sailed on to Japan and then to Shanghai.

Early Twentieth-Century China

When Jean Ewen arrived in China in 1933 it was just as lawless as America's old Wild West, if not more so. It was a country of catastrophe. Its inhabitants made up one-fifth of the world's population. Its traditions echoed feudal Europe, its peoples divided into rigid social strata: the scholar-landlord-merchant class, the military, and the peasantry. Industrialism was in its infancy. Famine, floods, pestilence, and insect plagues afflicted the land with biblical ferocity. In many parts of the country, landlords and tax collectors preyed on the poor, bandits prowled the rural areas, and pirates lurked in the waterways.

Political events were also coming to a boil in China. Nationalist hero Dr. Sun Yat-sen had died in 1925. The nationalist Kuomintang (KMT) under the dictator Chiang Kai-shek had split off from the communists in 1927, launching a struggle that would last until 1949 except for a brief halt during the Sino-Japanese War. In September of 1931, Japan had seized the northeast province of Manchuria. Chiang Kai-shek, supported by western nations, did little to stop the invading Japanese. He was more interested in defeating the so-called Red Bandits.[9] In 1931 he launched a series of Bandit Suppression Campaigns against the communists. On January 29, 1932, Japan had attacked Shanghai, and in February installed a puppet regime in Manchuria. All of this stirred up peasant discontent.

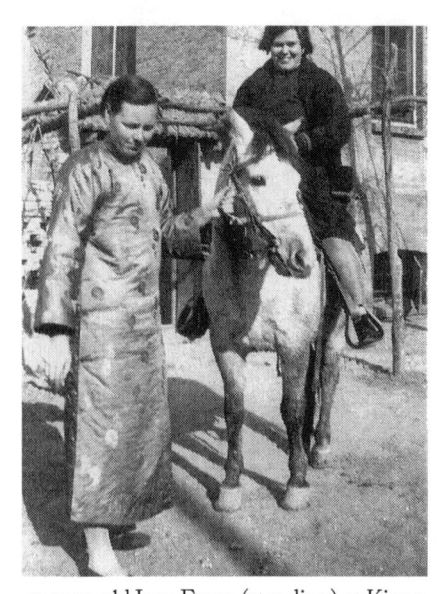

23-year-old Jean Ewen (standing) at Kiang Kia, Wutingfu, Shantung Province, ca. 1934. – *Photo PH 2000-83-3 from private collection of Tom Kozar, courtesy of Saskatoon Public Library Local History Room.*

Into this uproar rode young Jean Ewen from Saskatoon and her nursing chums, undaunted as only the young can be. At Shanghai, they boarded a coastal steamer heading north to Tsingtao[10] in Shantung province (now Shandung). A train bore them to Changtien, where they stayed at a mission compound, worked in a dispensary, and studied Chinese together. Next they were posted to Kiang Kia, one hundred kilometres north on the Yellow River. Quick-witted young Ewen picked up the local Mandarin dialect the fastest of the three and before long was sent out on her own. Before Easter 1933, she learned she was to be transferred to Chu Li Chang, an old village fifty kilometres east. Thus she found herself a lone Canadian in strange and chaotic surroundings that might have terrified a more timid spirit. There she first encountered a "witch doctor." She did not think much of his charms of chicken bones and feathers.

In 1934 the communists made their epic Long March to the Northwest. In June 1935 Ewen was again uprooted and transferred to a dispensary at Kuotown, a community plagued with syphilis and harassed by bandit raids. In one dramatic incident, she was kidnapped by bandits and taken to their leader's home to tend to his pregnant wife, who had suffered repeated miscarriages. Ewen nursed her sickly patient through to term, delivered her of a live *wa-wa* (infant), and the grateful bandit halted his raids on the community.

The Yellow River, known as the River of Sorrows, flooded a vast area in 1935, and foreign medical personnel were called to work with international famine relief and the League of Nations Epidemiological Unit. Disease was rampant: typhoid, cholera, leprosy, tuberculosis, even plague – from 1932 to 1945, Japan reportedly killed 260,000 Chinese with biological weapons, chiefly plague.[11] Western advances in combating disease, improved sanitation, and antiseptic methods all helped save lives.

Had Ewen been sent to work in a nationalist army hospital, her role as a nurse might have been shockingly different. Dr. Han Suyin, a famous Eurasian author and physician who grew up in early twentieth-century China, wrote that army nurses, after a hard day's work, were often forced at night to submit to lecherous soldiers, and thus were held in low esteem.

Missionary nurses in rural China were more protected. In the early thirties, missionary hospitals, funded from abroad, were the best-equipped medical centres. Foreigners were regarded as "turtles," "dogs," and "foreign devils," but a competent nurse like Ewen with access to modern medicines and supplies must have seemed heaven-sent. She did not push any belief system other than good health. She was practical, no-nonsense, and fluent in Chinese. When peasants ridiculed Ewen's "Big Nose" and unbound feet, she shrugged it off. To her, China was a challenging new frontier, exotic and awe-inspiring. She saw the country in all its tragic beauty.

As the Sino-Japanese War began, the three Canadian nurses opted to return to Canada in June 1937. As her service in China drew to a close, the Chinese government awarded Jean Ewen their prestigious Silver Shield in recognition of her service to the people of China.[12]

As a nurse at St. Joseph's Hospital in Sunnyside, Toronto, Ewen's life became more humdrum, but the tempo of her life was about to quicken again. Ironically, it was her father's Communist Party ties that harnessed her to the brilliant but temperamental Dr. Norman Bethune, who had recently announced he too was a communist. Ewen's nursing expertise and fluency in Chinese made her seem the perfect companion to accompany Dr. Bethune to China as his interpreter and nurse. Dr. Bethune had distinguished himself as a controversial and innovative lung surgeon in Canada before going to Spain. In the Spanish Civil War he had invented a new system of mobile blood transfusion units that delivered life-saving blood supplies to soldiers right at the front.

Had Ewen still been living in Saskatoon she might have met him in that city when Bethune crossed the nation in 1937. On August 23 he appeared in the Canadian Legion Hall on 19th Street East to screen a film about the blood transfusion programme in Spain and plead for dollars in aid of the cause served by Jean's brothers and her future husband.

The day Bethune appeared in Saskatoon, the *StarPhoenix* trumpeted news of the Japanese bombardment of the Chinese coastal city of Shanghai. Some four hundred people died and a thousand were injured when a department store in Shanghai was hit.[13]

BETHUNE AND EWEN IN CHINA

Ewen flew first to New York to meet Dr. Bethune. On January 8, 1938, they met again in Vancouver. They sailed to Japan, then Shanghai and Hong Kong. From there they flew to Hankow, a city on

Dr. Norman Bethune (right) with Dr. Richard Brown and soldiers of the Eighth Route Army, Northern China. – *Photo PA-116874 courtesy of National Archives of Canada.*

the Yangste River, and met Chou En-lai, then minister of war and later premier of China. Ewen's beaming face appeared in the Vancouver *Province* with a caption announcing that she had "reached Nankow [sic], temporary Chinese capital, recently on her mission of mercy." [14]

Although Bethune would have liked to establish mobile blood units as he had in Spain, lack of electricity, poor roads, and vast distances made that unworkable. It was decided they should join a Red Cross unit in the Eighth Route Army. The United Front agreement required that the Red Cross send medical teams into the communist-held areas, and an integrated system linking hospitals and an ambulance service was urgently needed to save the lives of the wounded. When Bethune asked Ewen if she would go, she agreed. As transportation to Hong Kong had been disrupted, their supplies would follow later.

Bethune relied on Ewen's language skills considerably, as he spoke no Chinese. English was widely spoken only in the major cities by the Chinese gentry and its mandarins. (Since the Opium Wars of 1839 Britain had spread its colonialist tentacles in China.)

First they went to Hanyang, a city nestled against Hankow. It was Chinese New Year and the Japanese were bombing the cold, damp city clogged with refugees. When sirens shrieked the two Canadians took refuge, but as soon as the raid subsided they began collecting medical equipment and supplies. Near the end of February 1938 the two left Hankow on the Blue Empress train, hurtling through Honan province to Chengchow on the Yellow River. There, the Lunghai train, on a line that crossed the country east-west from the coast to Lanchow, was crammed full and left without them. The duo rested in a freight shed until another train chugged along heading northwest. They arrived in Tungkuan (also spelled Tungchuan or T'ungch'uan) down the Yellow River from Sian and were sent to Eighth Route Army barracks.

Next they waded across the icy waters of the flood-swollen Yellow River, and hunkered down in a boxcar on the Tung Pu line train. Twice they were jolted from sleep by Japanese bombardment. When they finally reached their destination, Linfen, on the twenty-sixth, the Japanese were only fifteen kilometres away. They learned that the communist army headquarters had moved and they'd have to return to Tungkuan. But their train was not returning there. After their luggage and supplies were loaded onto another train, the two slept fitfully atop rice sacks. Before long the panicky engineer deserted the locomotive and they were marooned at Goasi, watching helplessly as Japanese airplanes bombed nearby villages. While their train's cargo was being reloaded onto wagons, Dr. Bethune dressed soldiers' wounds. But their caravan of forty wagons presented an enticing target. Two Japanese bombers dropped their deadly cargo, slaughtering several animals. One bomb exploded near Ewen, but miraculously she was unhurt. Upset by the bloodbath, Bethune and Ewen had an insult-hurling spat, and Ewen withdrew in tears.

Travelling by night, they reached the city of Kiang Chow, where people thronged to their inn for medical attention. With tempers as short as their supplies, Ewen and Bethune had another set-to. Bethune said: "You are truculent, self-sufficient, overconfident, and absolutely no use to me," and that she was "a disgrace to [her] illustrious father." But Jean would not kowtow to him. She retorted that she "always tried to be a disgrace to [her] father."[15]

For the present they were yoked together by their shared mission. Injured soldiers fresh from the battlefront had found no hospitals there. Bethune and Ewen were caught in the perilous zone between two warring armies, while their mobile dressing station attracted swarms of patients. Many Chinese had never seen a foreign "she-devil" before.

At Hotsin near the Yellow River, Japanese troops arrived and machine-gunned them on the Shensi side. Ewen narrowly escaped a bullet as she leapt into a trench for sanctuary. Soon Bethune and Ewen were sheltered with twenty or thirty other people in a cluster of six caves. They waited four days for Eighth Army trucks to arrive. Feeling gloomy, Bethune confided to her about his estranged wife, Frances, and admitted his guilt in the failure of his marriage.

Near the end of March, Ewen and Bethune perched on top of a cargo-loaded truck heading to Sian. At Eighth Route Army headquarters they learned that news of their presumed death had been reported in the Chicago *Tribune* on March 12, 1938.

At Sian they met Chu Teh, commander-in-chief of the Red Army, sometimes called the Chinese Napoleon. With the League of Nations

Epidemiological Unit they planned to set up a medical unit to go to the front, and were given vaccination and inoculation supplies. They were to go north to Yenan and cross the Yellow River to the Wut'ai Mountains in Shansi to help the besieged army and its supporters.

At Yenan, Bethune was greeted with joyous fanfare. That night when he was summoned to meet Mao Tse-tung, Ewen insisted on going too. Mao welcomed Bethune with warmth and affection.

While Bethune was otherwise occupied, Ewen went to the nearby Chinese Red Cross hospital, installed in bomb-immune caves. The cave-hospital was well-equipped but lacked plumbing. The pair moved into their own cave dwellings, sharing them with mice and insects. Bethune's famous temper erupted when he saw the hospital conditions in which he was expected to work. By then, Ewen was tired of being blamed for bad news, and the doctor was assigned another interpreter. But the young new translator grappled clumsily with unfamiliar words and concepts, lacking the sophistication to translate properly. Thus Bethune was in the market for a new interpreter when Dr. Richard Brown arrived from the Canadian mission in Honan.

Bethune and Ewen were both so unyielding, it was inevitable that the shaky bond between them would snap. Some speculate that Ewen may have spurned erotic advances by Bethune, but it was more likely ideological differences or simply mismatched temperaments that provoked the split. The abrupt manner of their parting was typical of wartime situations. Bethune and Brown ordered Ewen to go back to Sian for medical supplies. En route to Sian she encountered two trucks stuck in mud, loaded with their long-awaited supply boxes from Hong Kong. An American naval attaché in Sian, Evans Fordyce Carlson,[16] accompanied her back to Yenan, where she found her cave dwelling had been emptied. Bethune had left, with Dr. Brown as his new interpreter. She had been with Bethune four and a half months. Bethune's diary claimed they left her behind because she failed to show up. But Ewen saw it as a rejection, believing that he resented her sharing the glory of his mission.

Interestingly, Bethune later found a more submissive nurse. Kathleen Hall from New Zealand was connected with the Anglican Church Mission. She was running a little hospital on the border of Japanese-held territory in the Wut'ai Mountains, where the Eighth Route Army was battling the Japanese. Bethune wrote in his diary, "I have met an angel, Kathleen Hall...."[17] He often sent her to Peking (now Beijing) to bring medical supplies through Japanese lines. Later Hall was captured by the Japanese, who torched her hospital and deported her, but the slippery Hall disembarked in Hong Kong and continued her war work.

Alone Again

At least one source says that Ewen remained as head nurse at the hospital in Yenan, but her own account says she set off two days later northeast toward occupied Shansi, along with twenty-five students sent to educate the peasants. After a two-week stop at a hospital supply station in Ching Chan (possibly called Chingchien now) Ewen reached the rear hospital of the 120th Division, where the nurses, or "dressers," were all adolescent boys.[18] She taught them how to dress wounds, and the team organized measures to combat flies and dirt and developed an inoculation program. It was not easy to change peasant traditions. In parts of China, including the northwestern provinces, as journalist Edgar Snow noted in 1936, illiteracy was the norm and people thought water was bad for them (which it may have been, without boiling). In those areas, a man normally only had a bath twice in his lifetime, once when he was born, and once when he got married.

Jean Ewen article from *China Salvation Times*, 20 October, 1938. – *Photo PH 2000-83-8 courtesy of Saskatoon Public Library Local History Room.*

In mid-June 1938, Ewen rode by truck to Eighth Route Army headquarters. At Shui Teh two upsetting letters awaited her. One was from Bethune, urging her to return to Canada; he claimed she was too young for the rigours of wartime China. Another, from Madame Chiang Kai-shek, said she could only work in China under Madame Chiang's command.

But Jean was not so easily intimidated. She wrote a saucy reply to Chiang's aide, indicating that Madame Chiang would have to come for her personally. Then she ripped up the two infuriating letters. She was confident that the country's war wounded needed her medical skills.

Ewen continued to crisscross the region, the Japanese nipping at her heels. At least once she ran the blockade carrying medical supplies. Travelling as the lone woman in a convoy of soldiers, dressers, and pack animals, she arrived at Lanhsien city, near the Yellow River, in late June 1938. There she met the fearsome Ho Lung, division commander of the Eighth Route Army. She evidently charmed this former bandit, who had led armed peasant revolts before he joined the communists. Her early ranch experience came in handy when Ho challenged her to ride his stallion. It had never been ridden before by a woman and staged a tantrum, but eventually calmed down and clattered to a stop with Ewen still firmly aboard. Impressed, Ho then showed her horses that had been trained to lie down on signal.

Ewen was put to work in Ho Lung's medical centre. With medicines scarce, the army medical corps sometimes used native remedies such as opium. Jean helped write a medical procedures manual and set up a sanitation campaign, a bath house, and a service to rid people of lice.

What finally undermined Ewen's steely resolve, along with failing health, was an experience at the town of Si Mah Pu, where they blundered into the physical remains of a gruesome massacre. The town reeked of rotting corpses, and the church was smeared with feces. It was too much for even this hardened war nurse.

Heading for Home

By this time she was losing weight due to her poor wartime diet. Ewen was exhausted, and she decided it was time to go home. She began to wend her way back to safety one morning in September. But her exodus from the embattled area was to be even more spine-tingling than her trek north with Bethune had been. Her nomadic childhood had prepared her for this – abandoning places and possessions while racing across China's vast expanses, always one step ahead of the advancing Japanese Imperial Army. For the rest of her life, Ewen "never became attached to material things," her daughter recalled. "She used to say 'one bomb and it's gone.'"

It was a rough ride atop bags on a mail truck to Yenan, then in a Red Cross truck to Sian, where she encountered Dr. Brown, whose budding friendship with Bethune had been shipwrecked on the rocks of ideology.

A flood of Japanese troops was arriving in China, and there were fierce clashes in nearby territories and non-stop air raids. Canton on the south coast had fallen to the Japanese. The Sian-Chengchow line was under Japanese bombardment, but Ewen took what turned out to be the last train from Sian and arrived safely in Chengchow.

On October 17, 1938, Ewen took a chance that Hankow had not yet fallen and flew in a bullet-pocked plane to the city, which was now a jumble of barbed-wire defences. At Eighth Route Army headquarters, everyone was hurriedly preparing to flee further west as the Japanese drew near. Chou En-lai arranged for Ewen's exit with a couple leaving immediately on an army boat.

When an air raid siren sounded, the three took refuge in a lumber-yard and watched as Japanese bombs killed eight hundred civilians. Afterwards, carrying only a small suitcase and a purse, she boarded the rickety army boat to escape from Hankow. The ship, loaded with more than a hundred Chinese, chugged along in the darkness, mooring each morning under a canopy of foliage.

On October 21, Ewen and her companions went ashore for the day. She left her purse and other belongings on the boat – a mistake. As they returned that afternoon, they had to race for cover as three fighter planes zoomed toward the boat, scoring two direct hits. The boat burst into flames and its hull splintered apart; she heard the shrieks of wounded passengers. Bullets and bombs rained down upon them, and after an oil tanker was bombed the river was aflame. Again she narrowly avoided bullets streaking past her. The bombardment left only thirty passengers, twenty of them wounded. Their possessions lost, they had only the clothes they were wearing.

Ewen continued to trace a serpentine path trying to get out of China in one piece. Her bedraggled party trekked through swamps teeming with bandits, travelling in sampans and other boats, on foot, and finally in an ambulance. Arriving at last at Eighth Army headquarters in Changsha, they met at 3 a.m. with Chou and prominent American activist Agnes Smedley.[19]

In mid November, three days' travel brought Ewen and her friends to Hengyang, where they heard that Changsha had just been torched by patriots to avoid Japanese occupation. Next day an army truck took them to the city of Kweilin, where she left her companions and caught a ride in a car leaving for French Indochina (part of which is now Vietnam). On November 19, 1938, they raced away from Kweilin with the city under attack by enemy bombers.

On November 20 Jean arrived in French Indochina, boarded a ship leaving for Hong Kong, and on arrival found a hotel room. She napped, bathed, and revelled in middle-class comforts. Shortly she booked passage on a steamer that skirted the coast to Shanghai, where she saw a copy of the *Shanghai Times* with a photo of herself clad in a Red Army uniform.

RUNNING THE BLOCKADE

But Jean's plan to return home still slipped from her grasp. Dr. Sheng, chief medical officer with the communists' New Fourth Army, asked her to go on another mission to collect clothing, bedding, and medicines and convey them to Anhwei province, a dangerous trip behind enemy lines. Reluctantly she agreed to go. She was to travel with a newsman, a soldier, and Dr. Sheng. In early January 1939 they sailed on an Italian ship flying Mussolini's flag, and the Japanese let it pass. From the port of Wenchou they lugged their cargo inland. En route, the military police checked their phony ID which had been prepared by Chinese partisans. The notoriously brutal anti-communist governor interrogated them, but somehow her group managed to pass scrutiny. They continued into the New Fourth Army district and on to Tai Ping west of Shanghai, having circled south and north again to run the blockade. Tai

Ping had been levelled. The group plodded on foot through dense bamboo forests and by raft to southern Anhwei (later Anhui) province, where Agnes Smedley was based at an army hospital housed in a family temple.

One of Ewen's most grisly escapades took place when the medical team needed a human skeleton for teaching purposes. Chinese peasants thought a mutilated body would prevent them from joining their ancestors, and the Japanese usually recovered their own war casualties. So, one foggy night she and three Chinese colleagues dug up five infants' graves and found some serviceable bones, from which Dr. Chang reconstructed a tiny anatomical model.

Ewen was eager to leave, but Smedley coaxed her to stay on. It was hard, relentless work, the place swarming with war orphans. Some grew up to be Communist Party leaders, and Ewen thought the lack of parental love made them stern and unyielding.

On March 5, 1939, Japanese bombs smashed most of the village of Yen Ling, where Jean was working, but again she escaped unharmed. She turned down another project that involved running the blockade again.

She was saddened when an English-language radio station broadcast the news of the fall of Madrid in Spain where her brothers were fighting. She wanted to go home. The trio finally arrived at the refugee-choked coastal city of Fuchow, now in flames. Leaving in darkness, they sailed to Shanghai without mishap.

Home to Canada

In the winter of 1939, Ewen finally embarked for Canada. She left Shanghai on the *Empress of Japan*, the last CPR boat out. On it she spotted Dr. Brown, headed for Japan; he avoided eye contact with her. When her ship docked in Japan she did not go ashore, but Japanese soldiers pounded on her door and rudely questioned her. In spite of that, Ewen arrived safely back in Vancouver.

After the war other Canadian, British, and Australian nurses whose wartime contributions paralleled Ewen's were showered with honours and medals, but none were forthcoming for Ewen. Possibly Allied military officials did not know of her courageous exploits, performed as they were in faraway China with no other westerners present to witness them. More likely, such honours were denied her because she was the daughter of a Canadian communist. Her association with Mao's forces in China was another black mark against her, even though she herself was rather apolitical. Since then Dr. Norman Bethune has been acclaimed for his heroism despite his professed communist ideals, while Canadian history has virtually ignored his nurse, Jean Ewen. Despite their spats, Jean spoke highly of the doctor as a great humanitarian who was particularly touched by the plight of hungry children.

On her return, Ewen went to Toronto to visit her brother Jim, now returned from the Spanish Civil War. There she met and married his comrade-in-arms, John Kozar, who had been an ambulance mechanic in Spain, attached to the mobile field hospitals. Their first child, Laura, was born in Toronto in September of 1939. Their second child, Tom, was born in early 1942, eight days after Jean's husband, now a merchant seaman, perished off the coast of Newfoundland on a voyage to Mermansk.

On October 13th of that year, Jean, her baby Tom, her father Tom, and her brother Bruce, appeared in a photo in the Toronto *Daily Star*.[20] The article paid homage to Jean's exploits with Dr. Bethune, noting that she also served with the Chinese Red Cross and worked behind the Japanese lines with "guerrilla detachments." It also mentioned her late husband and her brothers, Bruce and James. An extraordinary family indeed. Ironically, her daughter Laura later mused that Jean was just like her father. Indeed, Jean's actions in China show she inherited his audacity, self-confidence, and spunk, but especially his passion for social justice. Jean's son, Tom, commented: "She was tough as nails, but tender as a rose petal."[21] Ewen showed her tenderness through nursing. Her compassion was particularly aroused by children and unmarried mothers, said her daughter, also a nurse.

Jean moved west in January of 1944 to the Okanagan valley. In 1946 she married Mike Kovich, with whom she had her third child, Michael,

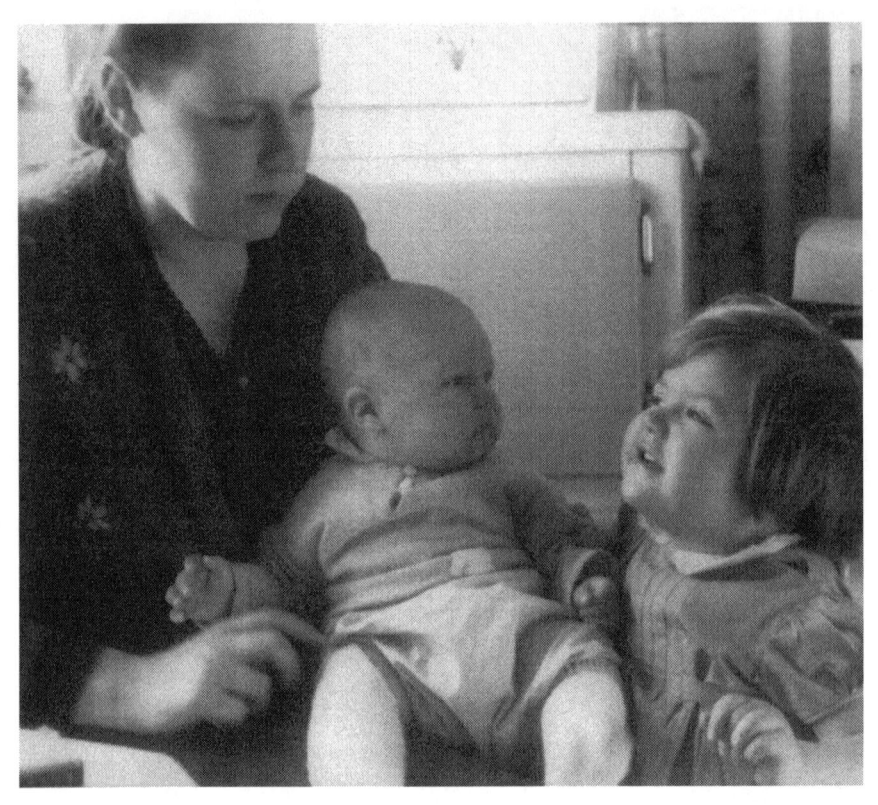

Jean Ewen Kozar with two of her children, Tom and Laura, 1942. – *Photo PH 2000-83-9 from private collection of Tom Kozar, courtesy of Saskatoon Public Library Local History Room.*

in 1948. The family resided in Penticton and at Okanagan Falls, later moving to Burnaby on the coast. Finally Jean relocated to Victoria, where she spent the last ten years of her life. She chose to spend her last days in the Victoria Chinatown Care Centre, among the Chinese she loved so dearly.

The launch of Jean's book, *China Nurse*,[22] in 1981 brought her brief celebrity. She was twice interviewed on the CBC in August 1976 in connection with opening ceremonies for the Bethune Museum in Gravenhurst, Ontario. She diplomatically avoided any negative remarks about the eminent doctor and spoke instead of his legacy.[23] By then she was in a wheelchair because of osteoporosis. In 1985 Ewen achieved a long-time ambition and returned to her beloved China with Laura to see how people were being fed and clothed. She suffered from vascular problems, and about three years later she died from kidney failure.

The Chinese Honour Ewen

After her death in Victoria on October 31, 1987, in accordance with her wishes, Tom, Laura, and two of Jean's granddaughters carried Jean Ewen's ashes back to China. In Beijing they stayed in the former home of Chiang Kai-shek. The twelve-car funeral cortege drove to Tangxian county, where some five hundred nurses, doctors, soldiers, and local citizens greeted them with spirited applause. At the memorial ceremony an official said, in part:

> For nearly two years, fearing no difficulties or dangers, she [promoted] Sino-Canadian friendship.... [We should] learn from her utter devotion and [emulate] her noble qualities of working hard and enduring hardships. We must emulate...her lofty international spirit.[24]

The convoy then drove in the rain (a good omen to the Chinese) to the Jincheng Mauseoleum of Martyrs in Shijiazhuang, also known as the Revolutionary Martyrs' Cemetery, forty kilometres from Baoding in Hobei Province, northern China. There the family noticed a statue of Norman Bethune near where her ashes were placed in a ground vault. When Laura noticed how close her mother's last resting place was to Dr. Bethune's, she observed, "Uh-oh, I don't think Mother would like this." But one of Jean's family quipped: "Naw, she'd just say, 'Move over Norman, I'm back!'"

Gladys Arnold as young woman. – *Courtesy University of Regina Archives.*

GLADYS ARNOLD
War Correspondent

In a haze of cigarette smoke, Gladys Arnold lounged with her friends in Regina cafés, talking of Life and debating the great social issues of the thirties. What bundle of beliefs would save their troubled world: socialism? fascism? communism? As the Depression's dust darkened the prairie skies and a more ominous darkness gathered over Europe, Arnold groped for answers. Clearly Europe was the laboratory for those "– isms." She must go *there*. The mission she was to embrace would introduce her to world leaders and win her international acclaim.

She was born October 2, 1905, in Macoun, Saskatchewan. Her father worked for the Canadian Pacific Railway, and the family moved frequently. She was nine when her father died, leaving Gladys, her mother, and her brother alone. After attending sixteen different schools, including ones in Calgary, Red Deer, Edmonton, and San Diego, she graduated from Weyburn Collegiate and then the provincial Normal School for teachers. She then taught at rural schools, and for a short time at the Success Business College in Winnipeg.

An article by a female writer inspired Arnold to become a journalist herself. In April of 1930 Arnold became editorial assistant to editor D. B. MacRae at the Regina *Leader-Post*. In 1932 she was sent to Quebec and was swept away by the Gallic charm of the French-Canadians. That dip into another culture and a yearning for adventure sparked her desire to go to France. After working at the *Leader-Post* for two years, and three times breaking her engagement with the same fiancé, Arnold headed for Europe.

A SLOW BOAT TO FRANCE

In July 1935, with savings of five hundred dollars and funding she had cajoled out of the Canadian Wheat Board, she sailed for London on a grain cargo ship out of Fort Churchill. Churning out two thousand words a week earned her ten dollars from the *Leader-Post*, and she supplemented her income with freelance work. At first her articles were standard fare written for the women's pages, but her writing became more political as Europe grappled with the coming war.

In London Arnold met media mogul Clifford Sifton, who told her Canadian Press (CP) needed a reporter in Paris. She became its official correspondent, at fifteen dollars a week. She moved to Paris in December 1935. Although she spoke only English, she believed in living among the French and not wrapping herself in an English-speaking cocoon, so she took French classes at the Sorbonne.

In 1936 Arnold went to Italy and was alarmed by the harshness of fascism. Her CP dispatch on October 28 was headed "Canadian Woman in Italy Tense Under Fascist Rule...Ten Year Olds Learn to Handle Rifles...."[1] Her dispatch dated June 2, 1936, described instructions being circulated in Paris for using gas masks: "Cities and Citizens Equipped Against Gas from Air Are Routine in Europe."[2]

In Paris she turned down another marriage proposal, this time from a wealthy young man eight years her junior. She never did marry. "Who would want to marry a globe-trotter like me?" she later wrote.[3] A commonplace life, married with children, didn't appeal to her. Her suitor later joined the French air force.

Civil war had been raging in Spain since 1936. In February 1939 Arnold headed to the border and was shocked by the havoc and suffering she saw. She praised the French for their gallantry in rushing doctors and food to help save lives as thirty thousand desperate refugees crossed the frontier, and she described the "heart-breaking page Europe is writing into her history in letters of blood."[4]

OMENS OF WAR

Arnold noted omens of war on three trips to pre-war Germany, the first in the summer of 1937, when her luggage was searched and her notebook stolen. In 1938, she noticed factories constantly grinding out armaments, and was upset to learn of the manufacture of poison gas. Those articles she sent from Germany mysteriously vanished.

In Germany she spotted a wall map showing the extent of German influence and indicating their long-range plans. By 1950, the plan was to include all of western Europe; by 1960, it was to be all of North America, she later told a reporter back in Canada. "I stole the map, wrapped it in plain paper, and mailed it to a friend in Canada. The Germans must have assumed it was a calendar or something unimportant because it reached Canada and was published."[5] On September 1, 1939, German troops invaded Poland. France and Britain declared war on Germany two days later, followed shortly by the Commonwealth countries.

Among other women journalists with whom Arnold might have elbowed for scoops were correspondents Clare Booth (later Luce), who wrote for *Life* magazine, editorial writer Germaine Beaumont of *Le Matin*,[6] Suzanne Wunder of *Christian Science Monitor*, Eve Curie, daughter of the famous French scientist Marie Curie, and other well-known journalists.

Although as a journalist Arnold was often turned away or referred elsewhere, she thought being a woman was an advantage "because the man (usually it's a man) was less suspicious and more open with me." She almost always got her interview. But she also thought that women journalists had to "work harder, study more and expect to be taken less seriously."[7] One's status as a journalist arose not from gender, but from country of origin, British and American journalists being preferred. To her indignation, Canada was low on the totem pole, despite being at war, and even though isolationist America was still sitting out the war.

The news services already carried extensive reports by the foreign press corps in Paris, so at first she wrote human interest stories. She focused on the social impact of war, to help Canadians understand what their husbands, brothers, and sons were facing.

Germany invaded Belgium, Luxembourg, and Holland in May 1940, and pushed into northern France in early June, ending the eerie period known as the phony war (or the *droll* war, as the French called it) between the declaration of war and the start of hostilities in France.

Toward the end of May she wrote to her mother about reaction in her household to news of the surrender of Belgium. "I heard cries of indignation and anger downstairs – and my friend Irene came up the stairs three at a time – screaming – 'Leopold has betrayed us – the king of Belgium is a traitor.'" This reaction was common in France. In the same letter she wrote, "I think Paris is very well protected and...the anti-aircraft guns and gunners are so accurate...the defence is marvellous...." That was also a common sentiment. Later she was to warn Londoners about false complacency, reminding them that Paris had been in a similar trance just before the Nazi invasion.[8]

With French armies now battling at the front, one of the first questions Arnold investigated was how food supplies were being handled.[9] Then, curious as to how women were contributing, she toured workplaces and found France had its own Rosie the Riveter phenomenon. Women took over the jobs of millions of fighting Frenchmen.

When Germany invaded northern France refugees flooded into Paris, and Arnold volunteered to help them through the Red Cross. As trainloads arrived on the outskirts of the city, "Boy Scouts and Girl Guides took off the dead. The living were sorted alphabetically and taken to distribution centers."[10]

By June 9 the city looked deserted. In late June only 983,718 people remained in Paris of its prewar population of 2,829,746.[11] The roads leading south out of Paris were jammed with evacuees. Estimates of the exodus range from six to ten million people. German propaganda that masqueraded as French news reports added to the panic. So did the departure of the government, and reports of enemy paratroopers descending into Paris dressed in disguise so they could blend in with the French.

On the trains, she saw twenty to thirty people in compartments intended for eight. Children were lying on the luggage racks. Mattresses were piled on top of cars to stop machine gun bullets.[12]

By June 10, the Parisians had been issued gas masks. Unlike most foreigners, Gladys also had one, and she slept with it. The devices might have come in handy the following day, when Paris was mantled in clouds of black smoke that masked the sun. It seemed to foretell an apocalypse. Was it automobile pollution? A smoke screen? Later it turned out that the black particles came from the deliberate burning of petroleum facilities outside Paris by the French so the Germans couldn't exploit them.[13] Fuel sources inside Paris were preserved, though, for the use of people fleeing Paris.

On June 10, a convoy carrying men and equipment of Operation Ultra, the "greatest secret of the war," was attempting to flee but was slowed to a crawl, caught up in the masses that choked the roads. Spymasters and some seventy staff were bearing a replica of the German cipher machine, Enigma. They succeeded, and later crypto-analysts in London broke the German codes using Enigma and throughout the war intercepted Nazi messages. Had the Ultra convoy been captured and the secret disclosed, effects on Allied strategy would have been immeasurable.

As a foreigner, Arnold risked being imprisoned when the Occupation began, so she decided to take other people's advice and flee. Her American colleagues, on the other hand, were relatively safe, for the United States was not yet involved in the war.

NAZIS INVADE PARIS

An advance guard of Nazis passed through cities and villages urging civilians to flee so that the resulting traffic jams would block the flow of Allied military vehicles. Now the avalanche of refugees who had been passing through Paris from the vanquished north grew larger with Parisians fleeing in panic. Departures from Paris on June 11, 12, and 13 were estimated at 130,000 per day. Refugees flowed south in horse-drawn carts and wagons or in automobiles, on bicycles or on foot, toting food and belongings in baby carriages or wheelbarrows. Some even brought dogs and cows. Arnold and two friends tracked down a vehicle and a miserly quantity of gasoline and fled Paris at dawn on June 12, 1940. By evening her party had advanced fewer than five miles.

In Saskatoon on that day, the *StarPhoenix* blared news of local plans to raise funds to buy a tank for the French. In due course a tank bearing the name *De la Ville de Saskatoon* was donated to the Free French forces.[14]

On June 13, the Nazis were a twenty-minute drive away. Paris was declared an open city to prevent the destruction of one of the greatest architectural jewels of the European continent. A sergeant in an engineering section was asked to blow up the Eiffel Tower to prevent its continued use as a radio transmitter. He convinced his superior that this would be considered an act of war, illegal in an open city.

The Nazis reached the gates of Paris on June 14, and the surrender was signed at 7:25 a.m. A French military emissary agreed to German terms promising no French resistance, otherwise Paris would have been

Arnold in Paris. – *courtesy of University of Regina archives and Special Collections.*

bombed. On that day in Canada it was announced that twelve thousand unnaturalized Italians were about to be fingerprinted and photographed, many taken into custody, in a search for "Blackshirt" activity in Canada. The sixteen thousand enemy aliens of German origin had already been rounded up.[15]

Taking back roads whenever possible, it took Arnold's party five days to reach Bordeaux, normally a trip of twelve hours. In Bordeaux she learned the French government had signed an armistice with the Germans. "Premier Petain's announcement left them dumb. Officers and men broke into tears in the cafés as they learned of it."[16]

Arnold left her friends in Bordeaux and fled to the port of Le Verdon, where boats awaited fleeing Britons. The docks were a chaotic scene as people dumped their cars and grabbed a few treasured possessions to take along. Above, Britain's Spitfire fighter planes fended off German Messerschmitts.[17]

Escape to England

Finally a small Dutch cargo ship was bullied into accepting some three hundred refugees. Arnold was lugging along a typewriter, a suitcase, and a briefcase. The suitcase containing her only change of clothes accidentally dropped into the sea. The typewriter and her papers were more precious cargo. Somehow she scrambled up a rope ladder, balancing the briefcase and typewriter. "You don't think about being scared, you do what you have to do. You just climb the ladder."[18] Her remark is a metaphor for her ascent out of the hell that was France under bombardment.

A German plane zoomed down and strafed them, but no one was injured. Later a German submarine shadowing them apparently did not consider the little ship to be worth attacking.[19] Passengers slept in the coal hole, while wounded soldiers were stowed away below deck. There were few toilets, and the passengers had to wash with sea water.

She made it to England safely. In London, though she was almost delirious with fatigue, CP officials immediately put her to work reporting on her escape. London was a babel of languages with so many European refugees. While she was at the CP bureau, an air raid siren wailed, and she stampeded with other journalists to the safety of the basement, her first experience of the Blitz in England. A CP dispatch dated June 24 about her escape from Paris appeared in Canada under titles like "Miss G. Arnold Caught in Flow of Humanity Streaming from Paris" in the Saskatoon *StarPhoenix*.

An interview in London with General Charles de Gaulle was a pivotal event in Arnold's life. She drew this plum assignment because of her fluent French. It was Canada's first wartime interview with the general.[20] Why, she wanted to know, had France been so vulnerable, why had Paris fallen so quickly? He explained to her about the *Blitzkrieg*, Germany's revolutionary, lightning-fast, highly mechanized form of warfare, a grand strategy he himself had long been advocating to the Allies. The German forces had circled around the supposedly invincible Maginot line and surged through Holland, Belgium, and northern France (where Allied forces had been trapped and miraculously evacuated from the port of Dunkirk). He remarked bitterly that the Germans had capitalized on military insights from his own books.

De Gaulle had learned that Vichy propaganda was flooding both Quebec and France; the Free French were being labelled "criminals, deserters, traitors, and mercenaries 'in the pay of the British'."[21] He had sent his former secretary Elisabeth de Miribel, the daughter of a French general and World War I hero, to explain to Canadians, especially Quebecois, what the Free French movement stood for. He asked Arnold to contact her.

In mid-August CP officials in London ordered Arnold to accompany and write about a shipload of children being sent to Canada for safety while their parents stayed to devote themselves to the war effort. Arnold was devastated to be ordered home, but she dutifully boarded the ship. Her article about the "guest children" appeared under headlines such as "G'bye Maw, I'll Be Writing Soon: British Children Leave for Their New Home."[22]

On her return to Canada she continued to work for CP, describing what she had seen and learned, to offset propaganda spewing from the puppet Vichy regime put in place by the Nazis. She also tracked down de Miribel and joined her in promoting the Free French movement in Canada. Years later Arnold talked about French Resistance activity during the Occupation, including helping Allied pilots who landed in occupied territory. Nearly seventy thousand members of the Resistance died in Paris alone, she said.

To Arnold's amazement, the French expatriate community in Montreal was split on the issue. Many were influenced by Vichy propaganda. Their negative spin on the Free French movement had convinced many who saw the Vichy regime as legitimate, and a Vichy agent harassed Arnold and de Miribel.

In 1941 Arnold crossed Canada on a speaking tour under the auspices of the Canadian Institute of International Affairs to inform Canadians about the Free French movement versus the Vichy regime. To inspire Canadians to join the Free French she informed them that "the German-controlled radio in France has made a definitive drive to sabotage Canada. The international short-wave in Boston has done much to counteract this propaganda."[23]

Communication with those inside France was shaky. Arnold and her friends exchanged cryptic messages, with code words for key international players. For example, she called De Gaulle her "boyfriend Charlie." Only a few of those written messages got through.

During the war, radio messages of hope to those living under the Occupation were broadcast by the Americans and British. From Canada, the CBC's Beatrice Belcourt broadcast five-minute messages by Canadians to transmit to France via a strong Boston short-wave station. Her first broadcast told of Canadian efforts to help the French, sending servicemen and funds to purchase armaments. Canada was also training pilots in the British Commonwealth Air Training Plan with its Initial Training Schools and Service Flying Training Schools across the land, including many in Saskatchewan cities.

Arnold left Canadian Press in 1941 to help de Miribel set up the Free French Information Service, of which they became co-directors. However, CP continued to call on Arnold for information and photographs, and she resumed working for them after the war.

After the debacle at Pearl Harbor on December 7, 1941, Arnold and her colleagues felt crushed when the Americans did not break with Vichy. At one point de Miribel was arrested in New York and briefly jailed, even though American colleagues had insisted the Free French movement was immensely popular in the United States. As a Free French advocate Arnold did get to meet Eleanor Roosevelt, the wife of the American president.

ALLIED LANDING IN FRANCE: ARNOLD RETURNS

On June 6, 1944, the Allies landed in France. They entered Paris on August 25. At the end of October Arnold was invited to return to France by Georges Bidault, a former Resistance leader and minister of foreign affairs in the provisional government, to report on the aftermath of the Occupation.[24] In December she and a friend crossed the Atlantic in a banana boat. On the way, the last two ships in their convoy were torpedoed, but Arnold and her friend arrived safely.

Once more on French soil, Arnold was shocked by the war's toll. Shortages were horrific. Supplies of heat and electricity were meagre. The people were thin and wan, their clothes in shreds. Bridges and entire villages en route to Paris had been bombed to oblivion. But Paris itself was intact.

The French showed no resentment at the devastation of their country, she said; they knew it had been the price of liberation. In Paris Arnold was reunited with friends, but it was a bittersweet reunion; many others were missing, held captive in concentration camps, or dead – either shot or starved or dead of other forms of privation.

After the Liberation she travelled to Alsace-Lorraine and visited the Struthof concentration camp. In a room attached to the crematorium, she saw meat hooks in the ceiling. Gladys learned to her horror that prisoners who had tried to escape or antagonized the guards were "impaled alive on these hooks," and when they passed out, their bodies were burned. Later she heard her friend Frank Pickersgill of Winnipeg had died this way.[25] A former freelance journalist in Paris, he became a secret agent with the Special Operations Executive (SOE). Actually the official report of his death at Buchenwald says he and other SOE agents were *hanged* from these hooks, using nooses contrived of piano wire.[26]

Arnold left for home on a troop ship with hundreds of war brides. Listening to them, she knew their husbands had woven bright fantasies about life in Canada, and wondered how the brides would cope with reality.

GLOBETROTTING

"How do you keep them down on the farm after they've seen Paree?" Arnold did not return to Saskatchewan. After the war the Free French Information Service was attached to the French Embassy in Ottawa. She also did what any globe-trotting foreign correspondent would do – she continued to travel and write, while also working for CP. Through the decades and well into her senior years she travelled to England, Italy, Ireland, Capri, Spain, Greece, London, China, Yugoslavia, Sweden, Denmark, India, Japan, Australia, the South Pacific, Arabia, Turkey, Egypt, and of course France. She had no qualms

A globe-trotting Gladys Arnold prepares for take-off on Trans-Canada Airlines.
– *courtesy of University of Regina Archives and Special Collections.*

about travelling alone, but she preferred company. When asked how she could afford so much travel on a reporter's salary, she said "travel was a lot cheaper then and I spent my money on that instead of clothes, jewelry etc."[27]

Back home in Ottawa, in 1948/49 Arnold took classes in the humanities at Carleton College. She was a generous woman – in the 1940s when her rent was $20 a month, she spent $52.60 on Victory Bonds to pay for the war effort, and $10 went to Save the Children. Later in life, she established two scholarships at the University of Regina, one for journalists and the other for students of French.[28]

She joined many organizations, including the Canadian Women's Press Club (CWPC), the Canadian Authors' Association, and the Canadian Federation of University Women. She was president of the Ottawa branch of the CWPC in 1948. As a journalist Arnold was admitted to important political events like the visits of Sir Winston Churchill and the Duke of Kent, and a NATO ministerial meeting in 1963.

Honours Pour In

Arnold served as a part-time director at the French embassy until her retirement in 1971 after nearly thirty years of service. That year France named her a Chevalier of the Legion of Honour, a distinction given to few foreigners and even fewer women.[29] In June 1987 she returned to France for a reunion with the Free French volunteers. The following year she received a Canada Council Explorations Grant of three thousand dollars to write her memoirs. In addition to journals and datebooks she had managed to preserve from the wartime era, she had four battered suitcases containing two hundred letters smuggled out of France during the war.[30] In 1987, at the age of eighty-one, she published her wartime story in an autobiography, *One Woman's War: a Canadian Reporter with the Free French*. That year, a Toronto couple took out an option to make her story into a film, but they were unable to get funding to renew the option in 1988 and the project fizzled.[31] Where they failed, others succeeded more than ten years later. She also wrote a novel,

Arnold in her later years. – *courtesy of University of Regina Archives and Special Collections.*

never published. In May 1988 Gladys Arnold was honoured by the University of Regina with an honorary doctorate of laws degree.[32] She was a featured guest on CBC's *Front Page Challenge* on May 13, 1988.

Arnold died in Regina in September 2002,[33] but not before seeing herself immortalized on film. If Arnold had been an American, her life story would probably be dramatized in a Hollywood movie, but in Canada we excel in documentaries. Her story is now celebrated in *Eyewitness to War,* part of a video series about Canadian women of courage.[34]

Father John Claffey – *courtesy of Bernadette McLoughlin*

FATHER JOHN CLAFFEY
Defying the Nazis

It was the height of World War II, and Rome was under German occupation. Escaped Allied prisoners-of-war, fleeing Jews, draft evaders, and other anti-fascists in mortal danger from the Nazi and fascist militarists were streaming to the tiny neutral haven of Vatican territory inside Rome. By word of mouth they had learned of a network of heroic priests and others who worked to rescue fugitives. Father John Claffey, born in Ireland and for many years a Saskatoon resident, was part of that secret rescue organization.

At the helm was Monsignor Hugh O'Flaherty, a fearless Irish priest who lived in the German College behind the Holy Office. Officially, he was head notary to the Holy See, writing and signing decisions of the Holy Office. This 1938 appointment ushered him into upper diplomatic circles and provided priceless contacts and financial support for his war work.

O'Flaherty spent one fateful year during the war as a kind of special agent, defying the Nazis and fascists and thwarting their horrifying practices of torture and murder. O'Flaherty's disregard for rules and regulations made him just the right person to arrange Resistance activities of priests in Rome, some of which were against the rules of Vatican neutrality.

The story of O'Flaherty's escape network is so dramatic and compelling it was immortalized on film. Based on a biography called *Scar-*

let Pimpernel of the Vatican,[1] the tale evolved into the film *The Scarlet and the Black*,[2] starring Gregory Peck as O'Flaherty. In many ways the film accurately portrays what is described in the book, although as in most dramatized biographies, the truth is sometimes twisted for dramatic effect.

Father Claffey was part of that compelling saga. According to his obituary, Father Claffey was born September 21, 1913, in Clonaderig, County Offaly, Ireland. He was the son of Kieran and Elizabeth Claffey. His family included sisters Margaret, Lillian, and Kate and a brother, Bill, and some nieces and nephews. As a young farm boy he lived through a turbulent era in Europe: first World War I, then the Spanish flu of 1918, and in Ireland the war of independence and a civil war. By the time a shaky peace had finally settled on Ireland in 1921, John Claffey was in grade three. After primary school he was sent to a boarding school, from which he graduated in 1929.

Young John lived about a kilometre from the great monastery founded by St. Kieran at Clonmacnoise in the year 546. It became, Father Claffey said years later, one of the most renowned centres of learning in Europe. He felt it "beckoned to him" in a subtle way. First he taught school for a while, then stopped teaching to labour on the farm. In 1933 he met a priest travelling in Ireland who told him about a seminary at Lebiscy near Caen in France, run by the Fathers of St. Mary's.

Inspired by the priest to become a missionary priest himself, the young Claffey applied to the Fathers at Lebiscy, and they immediately invited him to France. Claffey had hoped to spend Christmas with his family, but the Fathers insisted he come at once. John Claffey did not spend Christmas with his family until twelve years later.

Near the end of December 1933 he departed from Ireland for the French seminary, located not far from the fateful beaches of Normandy where the Allies were to land in 1944.

In 1937, he was sent to the Gregorian College in Rome. His plan was to pursue degrees in philosophy and theology and then return to Lebiscy to teach. But history intervened when World War II broke out in 1939. Father Claffey was ordained to the priesthood in Rome on July 14, 1940, by Cardinal Tisserant who headed the College of Cardinals. The following day he met Eugenio Pacelli, Pope Pius XII, who had become pope in 1939.

Hitler's Pope

The role of the Vatican during World War II is still controversial, particularly that of the Pope. As the head of a church that spanned the globe, based in the Vatican in Rome, the Pope was in a sticky position. Whatever his personal feelings about resistance movements against fascism and Nazism, he maintained a position of impartiality to protect the church. While he was aware of the actions of priests in Rome, he could not openly approve them for fear of jeopardizing Vatican neutrality and placing its occupants in danger.

But during World War II Pope Pius XII used the resources of the Holy Office to gather information and co-ordinate aid to escaped prisoners-of-war and other fugitives and thousands of Italians displaced by the war. Under his direction air-raid shelters and vaults to house archival papers were constructed inside the Vatican, and shelter was provided for Allied diplomats.

Despite these good works, Pius XII's refusal to use his power to raise Catholic opposition to the Nazis' persecution and eventual mass murder of the Jews has been harshly criticized. In 1999 an explosive book by John Cornwall, *Hitler's Pope*, argued that when Pacelli negotiated with Hitler his 1933 "Reich Concordat" that crippled Catholic social and political action in return for absolute papal control over religious matters, he dishonoured the papacy and betrayed the Jews.[3]

In 1938 Italian leader Benito Mussolini enacted the so-called racial laws which deprived Jews of most of their civil rights, and demanded that all foreign Jews be expelled from the country. In June 1940 Italy declared war on Britain and France, thus joining Adolf Hitler's crusade to kill all the Jews in Europe. Jews were not the only people endangered by the declaration of war, however.

Prisoners of War

Italian prison camps were filling up with Allied POWs. In 1942 there were seventy-four thousand known British POWs in Italy. Many of them were to escape from prison camps or jump off trains bound for Germany and make their way to Rome.

By November 1942 the Allies had invaded North Africa in Operation Torch. Relatives of missing Italian POWs were besieging the Holy Office with inquiries, and the Nazis were scouring the city for opponents, especially Jews and anti-fascists, some of them Roman aristocrats. By 1943 the food supply in Italy was shrinking. As well, the Italians suffered crushing defeats at Stalingrad and El Alamein. But for Allied POWs there was hope of release as the Allies drew near.

On July 25 there was a vote of non-confidence in Mussolini, whom the king stripped of office and arrested. A new head of state was put in his place, Badoglio. On September 8, 1943, the Italian surrender to the Allies was announced by the commander-in-chief of the Allied forces in North Africa, American General Dwight D. Eisenhower. The next day the Allies arrived at Salermo, far south of Rome near Naples at the "ankle" of the Italian "boot."

But the war was not over for the Italians. While many of them celebrated, there had been no Allied armistice with the Germans and no Italian declaration of war against Germany, and there were German army divisions all over Italy. September 1943 to June 1944 was a period of extreme peril in Italy, and longer in the northern provinces where the Germans set up a puppet government headed by the deposed Mussolini.

Many Italian soldiers were executed and others fled in civilian clothing to escape that fate, as the Nazis considered them deserters. Many soldiers fled to their homes, some joined the partisans, and some were recaptured by the Nazis and remained for the rest of the war in German POW camps.

After the surrender, as Italian soldiers abandoned their posts guarding the prison camps, a flood of Allied POWs swarmed out of prison camps and others emerged from hiding to stream toward Rome. Quickly, the German army stepped into the void left by soldiers gone AWOL, and political escapees balanced on a tightrope between freedom and captivity, or even life and death.

EVADING CAPTURE

Many were the ruses fugitives adopted to escape detection. In many European countries political refugees hid in tunnels, or dugouts and trenches covered with leaves and branches; in crude shelters in the woods, sheep pens, and chicken coops lined with acoustic panels; in cramped hiding places inside cupboards and artificial spaces created by false floors and ceilings; in attics and basements of private homes; in brothels, churches, monasteries, and convents. Others pretended to be patients in mental asylums and hospitals, and medical staff used elaborate and sometimes risky tricks to make their "patients" appear ill.

Even caves served as hiding places. A Jewish doctor who had escaped from a labour camp was sheltered by a grateful *padrone* (host) in a cave he had prepared in his orchard, with stashes of food and wine nearby. Elsewhere in the doctor's travels, several families took shelter night and day in a large mountainside grotto to escape the shelling. (The doctor emigrated to Canada after the war.)[4]

Moving from place to place was always dangerous. Sometimes escapees were concealed in a cartload of vegetable produce or under a load of hay being delivered by peasants into the city. A foreign escapee's accent would instantly give him away. To avoid speaking, men would pretend to be asleep when travelling by train so they would not be questioned. Others pretended to be deaf and mute. Or when in danger they might stuff their mouths with food so that when they answered, their replies would be muffled.

In the cities, places of sanctuary included private homes, institutions such as hospitals, churches, monasteries, warehouses, and hotels. One device used in Rome was to create hidden rooms partitioned off with no inside door. Men were smuggled into the Vatican disguised in priestly robes. O'Flaherty sometimes traded outfits with the men he was rescuing. Later German agents also began to dress as priests and hoodwinked escapers in Rome by offering them hiding places. Instead the agents took their victims to the dreaded Regina Coeli prison in Rome.

By 1943 fugitives were swarming into Rome for sanctuary. In addition to Italian ex-soldiers, they included thousands of escaped Allied POWs, Jews fleeing from the Nazis, young men evading conscription or forced labour camps, and ordinary refugees simply fleeing enemy attack. The Vatican was a natural place to seek refuge because it was considered neutral territory. Before long, however, it was full to capacity. Monsignor O'Flaherty's clandestine rescue network found lodging in Rome for the fugitives in safe houses, or rather safe apartments occupied by Italians. As well as priests and nuns, the Roman escape organization included anti-fascists from all walks of life, even a count and a princess. In view of the constant danger, they all adopted code-names. O'Flaherty's was Golf, and Claffey's was Eyerish.

Although O'Flaherty thoroughly disapproved of the English because of Ireland's political struggles with Britain, because of their common language it was natural for him and his coterie of priests to work on behalf of English-speaking prisoners-of-war. Throughout World War II, these included downed pilots, secret agents, medics, radio operators, and others dropped by submarine or parachuted behind enemy lines – any serviceman caught by the enemy and interned. The organization did not confine itself to helping POWs; they also helped escaping Jews and other anti-fascists in peril.

Undercover Priests

To assist escapees, O'Flaherty's underground organization engaged in typical undercover work. An important activity was making up fake identification papers to help them evade questioning. But by far their most important and hazardous activity was to guide the fugitives to safe hiding places.

The *padrones* of such billets took even more breathtaking risks in providing refuge to the escapees. Recaptured POWs would be imprisoned and possibly shipped off to Germany, but under the rules of international law they were supposed to be treated humanely. However, those who sheltered them could be summarily shot. People who housed the fugitives were often caught and tortured to squeeze from them the names of people in the escape network and other *padrones*. One of the bravest in Rome was Mme. Chevalier, code-named "M."

Father Claffey is mentioned several times in Gallagher's book. Claffey's specific role in the organization was to attend to the needs of escapees in Rome. Smuggling food and supplies to their billets was his number one obligation. Food and supplies were financed by wealthy Roman supporters, English diplomats, British Intelligence, and the modest resources of priests themselves. Each night heavily laden carts rumbled into Rome with food from the rural areas in an operation organized by a Count Salazar, and a wily agent named May bought goods from the black market.

Father Claffey and a seminarian in the parlour. – *Photo courtesy of Bernadette McLoughlin.*

The Nazis were aware of this covert activity, and running supplies to the political refugees became more dangerous. Eventually money was carried rather than packages, to avoid telltale bulges under priestly garments or baggage that might be inspected.

Repeatedly, Father Claffey slipped out of the grasp of the dreaded Gestapo and SS officers. His friend Dr. Daniel McFadden of Saskatoon said: "He'd go into buildings and out the back door and the Gestapo would be following him."[5] This was a typical pattern in Rome, and there were many hair's-breadth escapes.

He signed an oath of secrecy that bound him to silence about his wartime activities, but he did admit, "As the war continued I had not just my own safety to think about but the safety of thousands of refugees and escaped prisoners."

One of the people Father Claffey helped rescue was Col. Derry, who became a pivotal figure in the escape organization. An officer in the Royal Artillery, he had survived the debacle at Dunkirk, fought in Syria, became battery commander with the First Field Regiment (the Desert

Rats) in North Africa, was captured in July 1942 at El Alamein, and had been a prisoner-of-war at Chieti with twelve hundred other officers.

When Derry first arrived as an escaped POW in Rome, Father Claffey helped to rescue him from the Gestapo by dressing him in clerical robes and whisking him past the Nazis into the safety of the Vatican. This was a hazardous mission because Derry was tall, fair-haired, and blue-eyed. He did not look Italian, nor did he have an Irish accent, which would have provided a measure of security as a citizen of a neutral nation. For him to be stopped and questioned would have been a calamity.

Guided by Fathers John Claffey, Owen Sneddon, John Vincent Treacy, and Borg, and occasionally by O'Flaherty himself, Derry visited billets where people were concealed. As many as four thousand refugees at a time were under the care of the Roman escape organization during the German Occupation.

The Partisans

The Roman organization was part of a vast underground resistance movement throughout Italy that fought with awe-inspiring courage until the Armistice. In her book *The Other Italy: Italians and the Resistance,* Maria de Blasio Wilhelm asserts that there were about 224,000 militant partisans in Italy toward the end of the war. Of those, 63,000 were killed and more than 33,000 wounded. As well, 15,000 to 20,000 ordinary citizens were murdered and about 5,000 wounded.[6] The Italian partisans, aided by Allied secret agents, radio operators, and paratroopers, engaged in sabotage and guerrilla warfare, blowing up vital bridges, railway tracks, port facilities, and enemy convoys. They played a key role in clandestine communications using the underground press, microfilm, and coded messages via wireless sets, telephone, and even carrier pigeons. One memorable episode in Rome involved microfilming a list of escapees and hiding it inside a baked roll to get it past German checkpoints.

Women and children also participated in the resistance, often acting as couriers on bicycles carrying vital information or supplies. Not just in Rome, but throughout occupied Italy, courageous families provided sanctuary to fugitives of all stripes, who were also sheltered by monks, nuns, and priests in their institutions. For their heroic efforts tens of thousands of resistance workers lost their lives; some were tortured; others committed suicide to prevent yielding information under torture.

At the time of Rome's liberation, 3,925 fugitives were in the care of O'Flaherty's rescue organization. They included 1,695 British, 896 South Africans, 429 Russians, 425 Greeks, and 185 Americans. The rest represented twenty other countries. These numbers did not include the Jews and other refugees under O'Flaherty's personal supervision.[7] The *Scarlet Pimpernel of the Vatican* does not discuss the rescue of Jews in any detail, but at the end of the book, the author mentions that O'Flaherty flew to Israel to arrange transfer of surviving Jews there.

Because of the extraordinary courage of resistance workers who struggled heroically during the war, only 35 per cent of the 45,000 Jews who were in Italy during the German occupation did not survive. In 1938 there were 47,000 Italian Jews (one-tenth of a percent of the 45,000,000 Italians) and more than 10,000 foreign-born Jews. When fascism fell in 1943, 37,000 Italian Jews and 7,000 foreign-born Jews had survived.

Many members of the Roman escape network received medals and honours after the war. O'Flaherty was named to the Order of the British Empire and received other honours from Canada and many other countries. Some received Military Crosses. Father Claffey and others were awarded medals of special commendation by King George VI, but the modest, soft-spoken, self-deprecating priest never picked up his British Empire medal, said Dr. McFadden.

Not all Italian priests exhibited such courage. Lt. George Paterson of Kelowna, British Columbia, encountered some who did not. Parachuted behind enemy lines as part of Britain's Special Air Services, he made a breathtaking escape from a prisoner-of-war camp and had to swim a river to reach safety. After the bundle of clothing he was towing on a miniature raft was tugged out of his grasp by the swift current, he ran naked to a farmhouse and appeared at the door clad only in a sheet retrieved from the clothesline. When he was taken to a nearby priest, the apprehensive cleric quickly rustled up some clothing and pointed the way to refuge in the hills. Ordinary priests could be forgiven their nervousness given the stance taken by the Pope himself. Other priests did not share anti-fascist sentiments. Lt. Paterson approached a second priest and asked for food. The padre glared at him and refused outright, demanding in a menacing tone that he get out of there.[8]

A PRIEST IN CANADA

After the war Claffey immigrated to Canada, arriving in Halifax in 1949. He journeyed by train to Saskatchewan and served first at St. Brieux while he was still with the French order. Other parishes in the diocese of Prince Albert in which he ministered were Hudson Bay and Tisdale. After spending two years in the northern forests felling lumber to build a church, he lived in a church basement at Hudson Bay. In 1955 he joined the diocese of Saskatoon and served in Biggar, Meecham, Prud'homme, Dana, Watrous, Young, Delisle, and Vanscoy. In Saskatoon he served as chaplain at Canadian Forces Base Dana and St. Paul's Hospital, and as assistant at St. Frances Church. Father Claffey lived for forty-eight years in Saskatchewan. In 1972 his niece Sister Maeve Guinan and close friend Dr. Daniel McFadden of Saskatoon accompanied him on a trip to France to revisit the seminary where Claffey had studied, but most of the building had been levelled in the war. On his return he lived

Fr. Claffey with unidentified companions. (Nov. 1978) – *Photo courtesy of Bernadette McLoughlin.*

in a downtown apartment block and subsequently in a small, sparsely furnished room in a hostel in St. Paul's Hospital. A deeply spiritual man with strong convictions, Father Claffey eschewed materialism in his personal life. It is said that his scant possessions consisted of a suitcase, mattress, and sleeping bag. When his friend and colleague Father Ron Beechinor packed up his possessions, there was but one box full.

Father Beechinor observed in 2002 that Claffey was "a restless person" always seeking a home. His career beckoned him to four countries, and in Saskatchewan, several parishes. He would return home to Ireland with thoughts of staying there, but always came back. "My involvement with him was to try and help him find some kind of home."[9]

Fr. Claffey and Dorothy Robinson. – *Photo courtesy of Mrs. Bernadette McLoughlin.*

Claffey died November 21, 1997[10] in Saskatoon at the age of eighty-four. Although the wartime cloak-and-dagger story had been revealed when *Scarlet Pimpernel of the Vatican* was published in 1967, because of his oath of secrecy Father Claffey had kept the secret of his heroic past from all but his closest associates. One of them was Dr. McFadden, who presented the eulogy at Claffey's funeral. Mourners must have been dumbfounded to hear for the first time the astonishing story of their modest priest's wartime heroism. In his eulogy, Dr. McFadden reminisced about Father Claffey's childhood in Ireland, his simple and humble lifestyle. McFadden especially lauded the priest's spiritual devotion, ethical convictions, and death-defying courage.

After the funeral McFadden was interviewed by newspaperman Art Robinson,[11] and Claffey's story of wartime heroism was made public. The wandering priest was laid to rest with his family at his ancestral home of Clonmacnoise, Ireland, his restless spirit home at last.

Joan Bamford Fletcher, ca. 1940 – *Photo from collection of Fletcher's sister, Madge Tibbenham, courtesy Barbara Campbell.*

JOAN BAMFORD FLETCHER
Sumatra Heroine

Even as a child Joan Bamford Fletcher showed a flair for leadership. Possibly a scrappy tomboy, she acquired an air of authority. Even hard-boiled Japanese soldiers and hostile Indonesian rebels heeded this tough-looking Canadian lieutenant when she barked a command. Yet she won respect and admiration, even from former enemies. Fletcher was strong of body, firm of jaw, and bristling with self-confidence. She was going to need all that to meet the challenges her life would present.

Joan was born in Regina in 1918, the daughter of British émigrés Bamford Fletcher and his wife. They emigrated from Lancashire in about 1906. She grew up with her sisters, Madge and "Buddy," on a dairy farm near Regina, where she became a skilled horsewoman. Her father's family had been prosperous cotton merchants, and the girls were sent to boarding school in England in the 1920s. Fletcher's character was moulded by the Sisters of Notre Dame Convent, who taught her self-reliance and filled her with a sense of social justice. She received further schooling at Les Tourelles in Brussels, Belgium, and also in France.[1]

When Fletcher returned to Canada she worked in the Regina office of the Prairie Farm Rehabilitation Administration (PFRA), and helped her father gentle his horses. But Europe still beckoned, and the outbreak of World War II offered a chance to return. She trained as a driver in the transport section of the Canadian Red Cross, and she took an intensive motor mechanics course in the Saskatchewan Auxiliary Territorial Service, a women's voluntary wartime organization.

Fletcher paid her own passage to Britain in late 1940 or early 1941[2] and joined the First Aid Nursing Yeomanry (FANY), reportedly at the suggestion of the Canadian woman who trained her in the Red Cross, a former FANY from World War 1.[3] The FANY began in 1907 as a women's mounted medical unit that rescued wounded soldiers from the battlefield and transported them to field hospitals. In the first world war they operated field hospitals, drove ambulances and army vehicles, and ran soup kitchens and canteens. In 1938 the FANY became part of the new Women's Transport Service.

Although uniformed, the FANY was considered a volunteer civilian service. The women were trained in first aid, codes and signals, marksmanship, and motor mechanics. Some served as mounted couriers and drove convoys. Others worked as technicians or administrative assistants for the Special Training Schools. Still others became interpreters, decoders, forgers, or guides for special agents. Some even became secret agents themselves, dropped behind enemy lines as part of Special Operations Executive (SOE) operations. The FANY provided cover for many SOE operations.[4]

During the war Fletcher was stationed with other Canadian FANYs at Montcrief House in Scotland, where she drove staff cars and ambulances for

Fletcher with three other FANYs during or right after WWII. – *From scrapbook of Fletcher's life, prepared by her sister Madge Tibbenham, courtesy of writer Barbara Campbell, Regina.*

the exiled Polish army. But after the Allied victory in Europe in May 1945 Fletcher's future lay in the Far East, where the tornado of war still raged.

Land-hungry Japan needed the resources of Sumatra and Java, two major islands in the archipelago of some thirteen thousand islands in the Dutch East Indies, which had been colonized by the Dutch for centuries. The islands' rich oil supply was vital to fuel Japanese ships and planes. (Before the war the United States had supplied most of the oil Japan needed.) Sumatra was also on a strategic commercial route. In 1942 Japanese troops defeated Allied troops in Sumatra and Java. By August the Japanese occupied a vast area of the Pacific that reached the Aleutian Islands near Alaska.

The clash of East against West in World War II has been called the Vengeance of History – a moral payback for centuries of European colonialism. The collapse of Holland stirred the people of the Dutch East Indies, now calling themselves Indonesians and hankering for independence. Japanese propaganda claimed they had come to free the Indonesians from western domination, in a master plan known as the Greater Asia Co-Prosperity Sphere.

PRISON CAMP CONDITIONS HARSH

Prisoners-of-war and civilian internees were subjected to scant food rations and medicine, polluted water, forced labour, brutal discipline, degradation, and even torture.[5] These cruelties have been attributed to *bushido*, the Japanese feudal code of honour, with its doctrine of victory or death. *Bushido* decreed that warriors commit suicide rather than submit to the dishonour of defeat, thus the Japanese despised prisoners who had allowed themselves to be taken captive.

About a hundred thousand soldiers and civilians were held captive in squalid jungle prison camps in the Dutch East Indies. Men and women were separated; children remained with their mothers, older boys with their fathers. There they languished for three years. The captives suffered from malaria, dysentery, tropical sores, and malnutrition diseases. They became emaciated, and some died.

By the spring of 1945 the Japanese were losing in the Pacific, and prisoners were hearing terrifying rumours (later found to be true) that the Japanese high command had ordered the extermination of all POWs if the Allies invaded Japan. Suddenly, in August 1945 the United States dropped the Bomb over Hiroshima and Nagasaki. It was such an earth-shaking event that it had the effect of releasing the Japanese high command from their code of *bushido*. The order to kill all POWs was not carried out. Japan officially signed surrender terms on September 2, 1945.

MOUNTBATTEN APPOINTED TO OVERSEE EVACUATION

So many ships had been sunk in the war that there weren't enough to transport everyone home right away. Many people were stranded far from home, including soldiers and POWs. Britain's Lord Louis Mountbatten had been appointed Supreme Allied Commander of the South East Asia Command in 1943. In 1945 his specific mission was to evacuate Allied captives and send the Japanese troops home. The FANY were called upon to help with this mission. Fletcher was among the first FANYs assigned to the Far East. Initially posted to India, she reached Calcutta in April 1945, assigned to the British Red Cross Welfare Division. The Regina *Leader-Post* later published fragments of her letters home during this period.

In May Fletcher left Calcutta on a hospital ship that crossed the Bay of Bengal and sailed through the Malacca Straits toward Singapore. Her convoy threaded its way cautiously in single file through mine-infested waters. Fletcher did not arrive in Singapore until V-J day, September 2. There, she travelled to prison camps to care for sick internees, and was appointed personal assistant to the brigadier in command.

The International Red Cross played a key role in supplying food and supplies to Japanese prison camps in World War II.[6] But in many Japanese prison camps those parcels were snatched by the Japanese, who were suffering extreme food shortages themselves. On their arrival in Singapore Fletcher's unit toured the ammunition dumps still under Japanese control. There they found "Red Cross supplies sent by Australia, Canada and Britain and about

500 Red Cross parcels. We took as much as we could back to camp."[7]

On September 7 the first food packages were parachuted in by air. In North Sumatra the Japanese did not announce their surrender until September 21; they had been ordered to maintain control there until Allied forces showed up. But the Allied forces were late in arriving to evacuate the prison camps. They did not reach the Dutch East Indies until September 29, 1945, so the 26th Indian Division commanded by a British officer was assigned to Sumatra.

The political vacuum between the close of war and arrival of troops gave ample time for Indonesian nationalists to declare independence on August 17 and assume control, with Sukarno as president. But Sukarno's government was not recognized internationally. Holland maintained its claim on the archipelago, despite the absence of its forces there.

Lord Mountbatten described the Japanese postwar legacy in one word: chaos. Indonesia, he said, was the worst. "There were horrible mutilations and massacres and ugly deeds on both sides."[8] Mountbatten's wife, Edwina ("Lady Louis"), had earned great admiration by rescuing POWs in Germany and was now chief superintendent of the St. John's Ambulance Brigade, chairing its coordinated activities with the Red Cross. In "Operation Mercy," Mountbatten sent his wife to the Dutch East Indies to assess conditions in prison camps, hospitals, medical centres, and convalescent homes. She toured the Bangkinang camp on September 16 with the head of the Royal Army Medical Corps, a major, and some staff, and spoke with most of the internees. Her report reflected her horror at camp conditions. In one civilian camp on Sumatra the death rate was reported at 37 per cent.[9] Doctors were brought over from the nearby prisoner-of-war camp to lighten the medical load.[10]

When belated news of the Japanese surrender was received at Bangkinang the situation was too dangerous for the prisoners to leave, with no Allied troops there to oversee their evacuation. Both the Dutch and the Japanese were eyed as alien intruders by the Indonesians. Youthful rebel groups, many of them trained militarily by the Japanese and bearing weapons, had begun a bloody struggle for independence. In parts of the Dutch East Indies unruly nationalists were attacking prisoners, mostly Dutch. It was crucial that the prisoners get out.

FLETCHER'S PERILOUS ASSIGNMENT

Lt. Fletcher's assignment was daunting. She was to go into the Sumatran jungle, locate some two thousand women and children captives in the camp at Bangkinang, and evacuate them safely to the port city of Padang on the Indian Ocean coast. Bangkinang is located near the centre of the island of Sumatra, north of Padang and southwest of Singapore, across the strait.

At war's end the role of SOE secret agents in the Far East shifted from sabotage and espionage to accepting Japanese surrender and maintaining order. Seven paratroopers of Force 136[11] of the SOE were dropped into Bangkinang to check out the situation and prepare for the pull-out of former captives.

On October 5 Fletcher went to Bangkinang prison camp. The former Japanese prison guards and their officers would suffer reprisals if the internees did not get out safely, so at Japanese army headquarters in Fort De Kock Fletcher was able to negotiate the use of Japanese transport vehicles. She was also given an armed guard of forty Japanese soldiers.

To communicate her orders, Fletcher demanded the services of interpreter Art Miyazawa, who had learned English in the United States as a child. A journalist, he was university-educated, a second-generation Japanese-American with a gift for languages.

The first convoy set out on October 12 with passengers in the lead vehicles followed by baggage cars and a repair car. The convoys stopped for five minutes every hour for the benefit of the women and children. They travelled along a zigzag route over the Equator through lofty jungle terrain. To reach the coast, the convoys passed through a chain of five thousand foot volcanic mountains that parallels the west coast. Driving a borrowed jeep, Fletcher served as troubleshooter as she and her interpreter roamed back and forth along the columns. The length of the journey was variously reported as 280, 300, 500, or even 900 miles (450-1500 kilometres). The latter reports may have counted the mileage Fletcher's jeep logged going back and forth. Each trip took about twelve hours one way, after which Fletcher raced back to accompany the next convoy.

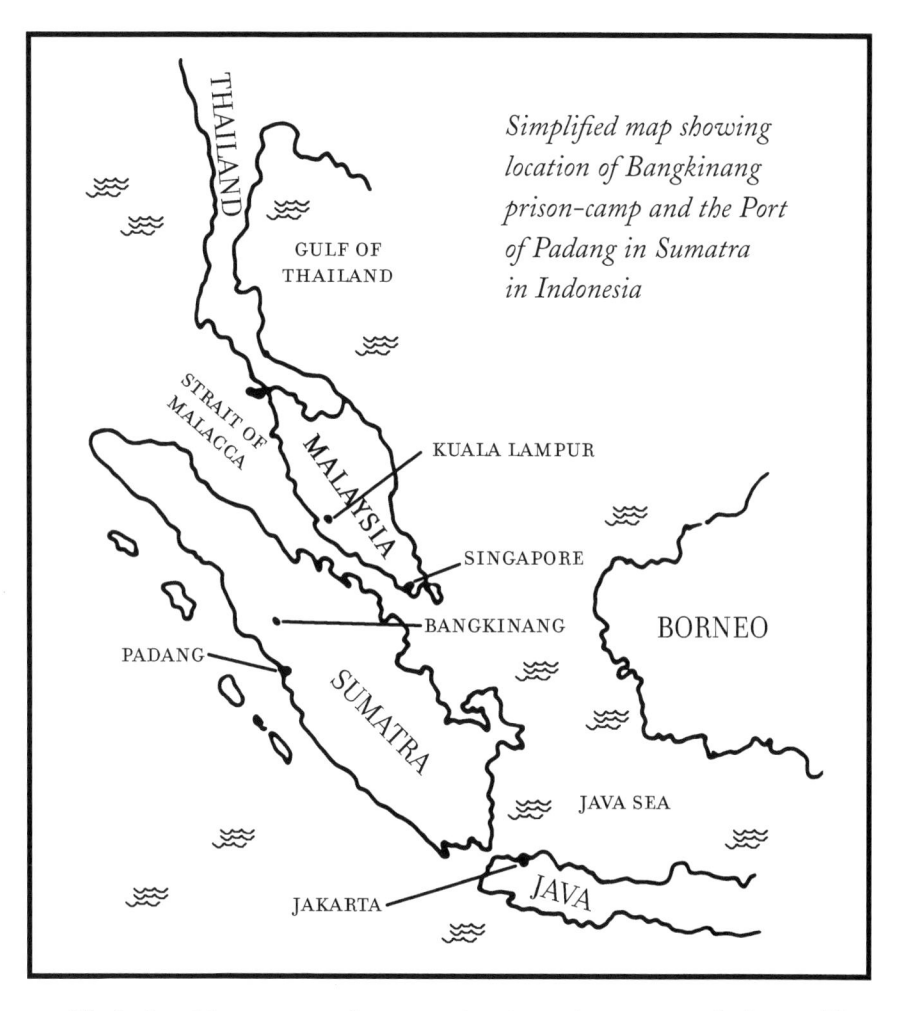

Simplified map showing location of Bangkinang prison-camp and the Port of Padang in Sumatra in Indonesia

Their first hiccup was a ferry crossing in early morning darkness. The engineless ferry was powered by a boy jumping on a cable that spanned the river; his actions jerked the craft across with the current. When the convoys came to blown-up bridges, the passengers improvised boats to get the trucks across the rivers. The worst was at Rantan-Brangin. If a bridge was damaged but intact, the people would gingerly walk across, wait for the trucks to rumble across the swaying bridge, and then clamber back into the trucks.

Lt. General Moritake Tanabe fretted that his men, humiliated by defeat, might commit *hara-kiri* by hurtling over the cliffs with their prisoners, but their will to live prevailed.

"It shook the Japanese a bit to find themselves under the command of a woman," Fletcher told reporters later. The anomaly of a lone woman commanding fierce Japanese troops was not lost on the press, who swarmed her on her return to the West. Photographs of this blunt, gutsy lieutenant from Canada began appearing in the western press, with headlines such as "Heroine Led the Japs, Saved Internees" and "One Woman Ordered: the Enemy Obeyed."

Once, Fletcher said, she was nearly killed when she was mowed down by a truck driven by an East Indian. "The edge of a truck wheel went over my heel," she recalled. "My coat caught in the wheel of the truck and I was dragged under. My [scalp] was split open four inches."[12] A Japanese doctor pulled the wound together and stanched the blood, and later an Allied physician stitched her up. Her companions urged her to rest but, undeterred, two hours after the accident she carried on with the evacuation.

Fletcher's grit and determination impressed the freed captives and the Japanese soldiers. After that episode, the soldiers saluted her when she passed. But some of the Japanese said they'd never marry an "Englishwoman," assuming they were all "too tough" like Fletcher.[13]

When the monsoon rains began each trip became more treacherous, as the convoys lurched around hairpin turns and vehicles were mired on roads now turned into muddy bog. When the rebels placed barricades on the road Fletcher directed that a "crash car" with a special bumper lead the column and plunge through the barricades.

On their second-last trip, Fletcher and a Japanese officer were leading the convoy in their jeep while a truckload of armed Japanese soldiers brought up the rear. After halting to fix a tire along the column, Fletcher returned to the front to discover that two Dutch passengers in the lead car had vanished, and an Indonesian was making off with the car. She pulled alongside it in her jeep, yanked open the car door, and bellowed, "Out!" The Indonesian hopped out and bolted. Fletcher and her interpreter went in search of the missing evacuees and she found them being held captive in a hut. One Indonesian was waving a knife, another wielded a gun, while a third was interrogating the two Dutchmen. Fletcher's shrewd interpreter insisted the captives were actually

British, while Fletcher shrieked and cursed. The Indonesians were stunned by the sudden intrusion of this large, forceful foreign woman. Her words were alien but her meaning was perfectly clear. Reportedly she grabbed the knife, slashed the rope binding one of the captives, and told him to "get going." (Presumably someone did the same for the other fellow!) Then she whirled and stomped out of the hut, inwardly fearing a knife in the back. By sheer bravado Fletcher's party escaped unharmed.

On the last convoy the rebels were so menacing her guard was increased to seventy Japanese soldiers with machine guns. But Fletcher thrived on peril. "It was fatal to stop," she later told reporters.[14] "I just loved every minute of it."[15] She made the crossing twenty times.

When Allied troops finally landed at the port of Padang, a British officer told Lt. Fletcher they would take over. Regulations demanded that she hand over the job to the Allied troops, but an obliging brigadier-general in charge of the troops let her continue, on condition that his commander at Padang not find out.

One of the finest testimonials to Lt. Fletcher's courage and fairness during the evacuation came from the Japanese themselves. In a grand gesture the captain of the Japanese transport company that lent their vehicles presented her with his three hundred-year-old ancestral Samurai sword because he was so awed by her courage.[16]

After the evacuations the Indonesian archipelago became a hotbed of competing political, ethnic, and religious factions. The bloody struggle for independence, particularly in Java, raged until the Dutch were ousted and independence was won in 1949.

By then Fletcher was long gone. After a week in Padang she flew to nearby Singapore. There she was asked to organize a unit to go to Hong Kong, where she flew at the end of November 1945. Three weeks later she was in hospital with a severe case of swamp fever. She returned to England in July, but the disease resurfaced, lodging in her jawbone. Half of her lower teeth had to be yanked out and part of her left jaw scraped away and replaced with plastic.

Fletcher as a FANY driver in Britain during World War II. – *From scrapbook of Fletcher's life, prepared by her sister Madge Tibbenham, courtesy of Barbara Campbell, Regina.*

Spies and Lies

But her adventures were not over. Fletcher had learned Polish as an ambulance driver for the exiled Polish army in Britain, so her next posting was with the Information Section of the British Embassy in Warsaw. One day in 1946 a telegram arrived from the British government announcing the king of England was naming her a Member of the Order of the British Empire for services in the Far East. The MBE medal was presented to her by the British ambassador to Poland. Journalists loved the story. *Time* magazine, *Saturday Night*, and several newspapers applauded her exploits.[17]

By 1946 the Cold War was heating up. As the Iron Curtain descended in Europe, Fletcher was now to experience the terrors of Stalinism. The Polish secret police claimed that a fifth column of former resistance workers was committing a wave of terrorism.[18] Suspicion focused on foreign embassies in Warsaw, which were thought to be sheltering spies and saboteurs.

In 1950 Fletcher was caught up in a political storm involving a former British attaché, Group Captain Claude Henry Turner, who had supposedly coaxed Barbara Bobrowska, a glamorous Polish redhead, to try to escape from Poland to Britain. Fletcher had reportedly laid the groundwork for this operation. She received a warning phone call telling her to flee from Poland because the communist secret police were after her. Horrified, she raced home and torched all the pages in her address book that might identify Poles she knew. Aware of her imminent danger, the British told her the RAF would airlift her out. This time she did not protest, for she knew people were disappearing.

The would-be emigrant Bobrowska was found with Turner on the British ship *Baltavia*, and three British men were arrested and charged with inciting Bobrowska to leave Poland illegally. In December 1950 Turner was sentenced to eighteen months in jail. Journalists suggested that the former attaché had been framed and that the redhead was herself a communist agent.

Joan Fletcher told reporters the secret police "trace you to every new address and search the place while you are out [and] every phone call is listened to. Friends and contacts come under scrutiny too...."[19] The Polish legation in Ottawa denied Fletcher's claims that she had almost been nabbed by the secret police.

BACK TO CANADA

When she learned that her mother was ill, Fletcher sailed to Vancouver, where her family were now living, to take care of her mother and raise horses. After the war Fletcher kept in contact with her Japanese translator, Art Miyazawa. When she died in 1979, he wrote to her sister telling of his recent reunion with the veterans she had led. "Virtually every veteran present recalled the tough but fair-minded woman lieutenant who amazed our troops with her consummate knowledge and

In peacetime, Fletcher relaxes with a friend on a sea voyage. – *From scrapbook of Fletcher's life, prepared by her sister Madge Tibbenham, courtesy of writer Barbara Campbell, Regina.*

expertise in handling the assignment at hand." The unit's honour roll of deceased veterans now bore her name, he wrote.[20]

Why would the Japanese bestow such an honour on a former enemy, a commander who was not really a soldier, and a woman at that? Miyazawa explained that Lt. Fletcher's actions had exempted his unit, the *Yamashita Butai*, from serving a year's hard labour in Malaya, the fate of many Japanese soldiers after the war. When their unit was shuffled off to Malaya, their C.O. whipped out a commendation signed by Lord Mountbatten, testifying to their "outstanding performance" in evacuating prisoners from Bangkinang. At once, the soldiers were shipped to Singapore and sent home on the next available ship. Miyazawa attributed the happy ending to his own foresight in coaxing her to write a testimonial on their behalf. He believed she passed her commendation to Mountbatten through her personal contact with Lady Louis.

His former superior Lt. Matsuo also wrote a tribute testifying to Fletcher's courage, concluding "perhaps she [has] no living equal."[21] He couldn't resist mentioning that it was *he* who had commanded the Japanese unit, although Fletcher had been "a responsible officer." A Dutch report also credited a Dutch sergeant named Braskamp for his work in arranging transport from the camp.

The 2001 documentary *Rescue from Sumatra*[22] commemorates Lt. Fletcher's heroic adventures, and a collection of her letters was being prepared for publication by Regina scriptwriter Barbara Campbell. Fletcher's Samurai sword is now preserved at the Canadian War Museum, a testament to her courage and integrity.

Emma Woikin, possibly in the mid-40s. – *Photo PH 98-113-5 from collection of Fred and Doreen Konkin, courtesy of Saskatoon Public Library Local History Room.*

EMMA WOIKIN
Doukhobor Farm Wife Turned Spy

A few months after the end of World War II, the western world was thunderstruck by Igor Gouzenko's revelations of a supposed spy ring in Canada. He is still remembered as the bizarre man with a bag over his head, worn to protect his identity and prevent the Russians from hunting him down for his disloyalty to the Soviet Union. Much has been written about the sensational spy trials that helped to fire up the Cold War, but until the mid-1980s little was known about the timid young farm woman who was caught like a careless bug in the web of Ottawa intrigue.

Emma Woikin was born December 30, 1920,[1] to Alex and Pearl Konkin and grew up on a homestead near Blaine Lake. They were members of the Independent Doukhobor community on the North Saskatchewan who had fled to Canada in 1899 to escape persecution in Russia. The Doukhobors survived their first hostile winter in Saskatchewan by living in caves dug into the hillsides.[2] At Ospennia in the Blaine Lake area the somewhat dilapidated family home still stands on their homestead on the northwest section, 2-44-6 w3.

Emma was the youngest of five children, a cherished "afterthought" child born to an aging mother. Some in the family suspected her real father was the hired man, whom she resembled and who left his estate to her. Even as a small child Emma was especially bright and had a phenomenal memory, a trait shared by some of her siblings.[3] She skipped grades in school and as a result was not allowed to go on to high school after grade eight because she was thought to be too young. Even in the harrowing Depression years, Emma's family life was warm, merry, and loving. She married her sweetheart, Bill Woikin, in 1937. They played the guitar and motored around the countryside, a blissfully happy couple.[4]

Emma Konkin as a teenager loved to play the guitar. 1937. – *Photo PH 98-113-2 from collection of Fred and Doreen Konkin, courtesy of Saskatoon Public Library Local History Room.*

Then calamity struck. Their only child died at birth, and Emma was unable to conceive another. Soon afterward Bill, in despair, hung himself. He may have suffered from depression or could not endure the pain of his frequent and intense headaches. In the days before free hospitalization and socialized medical care in Canada, it appears that he did not receive professional help, and for the rest of her life Emma blamed the Canadian medical system.

On to Ottawa

In order to stitch her shattered life back together, in 1942 Woikin decided to further her education by training as a stenographer at a convent in Marcelin, Saskatchewan. One report said Woikin started a nursing course in Saskatoon but didn't like nursing.[5] Woikin later testified in royal commission hearings that she had worked as a domestic in a lab there. Jobs were scarce, so at her family's urging she set out on her own for a civil service job in Ottawa. The clever young widow started in the Passport Office but soon got a job as cipher clerk at the Department of External Affairs, deciphering secret messages to and from the British. It was a strange place to put a Russian-Canadian. Even though the USSR was at that time an ally, the western nations still didn't trust the Russian Premier Stalin. The department's error later astonished Prime Minister Mackenzie King, whose government was raked over the coals in Parliament by John Diefenbaker in the hoopla to follow.

Emma Woikin in Marcelin where she attended secretarial school at a convent, 1942 – *Photo PH 98-113-8 from collection of Fred and Doreen Konkin, courtesy of Saskatoon Public Library Local History Room.*

Since the Bolshevik Revolution in 1917, Canadian communists – "the Red Menace" – had been persecuted and feared. When Stalin signed a non-aggression pact with Hitler in 1939, it got worse. Communist parties were banned in many countries. But in Canada anti-communism subsided temporarily during World War II after Germany invaded the USSR in June 1941 and the USSR joined forces with the Allies to defeat Hitler's Nazis.

Russian diplomats in Ottawa took special notice of the young Russian-speaking Doukhobor in the ciphers office at External Affairs. Of a sweet temperament but not glamorous, Woikin was wooed into Russian diplomatic circles. Her new Russian friends rhapsodized about the Soviet social system and praised its socialized medical care that had been so lacking in Emma's life.

At a dinner party on May 1, 1944, Woikin met Major Vsevolod

Sokolov, a handsome army officer at the Soviet embassy who reported to Nicolai Zabotin, a military attaché at the embassy. According to her biographer, June Callwood,[6] some thought Woikin was seduced by Major Sokolov. Or perhaps infatuation made her willing to comply with his audacious request – to pass along the contents of secret messages she had decoded. Woikin memorized the messages she decoded and later transcribed them almost word for word and passed them to Sokolov's wife, Lida. Like others later fingered by Gouzenko, Woikin was careful to pass on material that had already been reported in the public media or was not politically sensitive. She accepted a "gift" of money only once, to buy a train ticket home to her family in Blaine Lake.

In the Gouzenko hearings, when asked why she had passed classified material, Emma said she did it for love of her family's mother country, Russia. She felt there was "hope for the poor" and "security" in the USSR. Though not a member of the Communist Party, she had even applied for Russian citizenship. She told her interrogators that her baby died "because we had no medical care, and nobody seemed to care. My husband was sick and...nobody seemed interested at all."[7]

Igor Gouzenko

In July 1945 another young cipher clerk, Igor Gouzenko, Woikin's counterpart at the Russian embassy, found out he was to be repatriated to the Soviet Union. The war had left the USSR in a shambles, and its standard of living and freedoms could not compare to those in Canada. He loved the perks of being a diplomat in Canada, and he may also have feared for his safety if he returned to the USSR. He got a brief reprieve when he was ordered to train his recently arrived replacement, but he knew he would be forced to return to his homeland shortly.

During the war, scientists in the United States had been beavering away on the Manhattan Project. When they perfected the new atomic bomb, Roosevelt favoured sharing atomic secrets with the Russians; Churchill did not. Because of the edginess of the alliance, the USSR was denied access to the new technology. Canada was admitted to the atomic club because it had uranium, a uranium refinery, vast hydroelectric resources, and research labs far from the front.

When atomic bombs exploded over Japan in August 1945 and the war ended, the Russians wanted this cataclysmic new weapon too. They were also fascinated by Canadian progress in explosives, radar, and optics. Clearly the solution was espionage. With amusing cloak-and-dagger ploys they approached a number of Canadians in sensitive positions, people who perhaps innocently gave them information, although much of it was already available or easily obtained.

By September Gouzenko was in a panic. In a dramatic move, he defected from the Soviet embassy on September 5, 1945. He went to the Russian embassy after hours and seized a large number of papers that he had earlier gathered up or tagged to grab later and hid them inside his clothes. They implicated a number of Canadians in a so-called spy ring. While there he finished some telegrams, which had been his excuse for returning to the embassy after hours. He wrote in *This Was My Choice*[8] that some of those telegrams dealt with information obtained by Emma Woikin. He noted, perhaps ruefully, that those telegrams helped send "poor Emma" to the Kingston Penitentiary, along with several other people accused of conveying secrets to the Russians.

Gouzenko's efforts to expose the network of pro-Soviet spies were at first met by politicians and the media with almost comic disbelief and reluctance to get involved. As Prime Minister Mackenzie King told his diary, he was loath to have the government step in, as the case might anger Stalin and spark a third world war. Two likely outcomes if they did not step in were suicide by Gouzenko, or his assassination by the Soviet NKVD, precursor of the KGB. To prevent this, King sent two agents to watch the apartment house and grab the documents and other evidence. Terrified, Gouzenko saw the agents lurking outside the apartment and thought they were Soviet spies.

During the period between his defection and being taken into protective custody, Gouzenko and his family were truly in peril of being captured by the dreaded Russian secret police. The day after his defection, after failing to obtain sanctuary from Canadian officials, the

Emma Woikin in Ottawa where she worked as a cipher clerk in the Department of External Affairs, ca 1944. – *Photo PH 98-113-3 from collection of Fred and Doreen Konkin, courtesy of Saskatoon Public Library Local History Room.*

Gouzenkos took shelter in a neighbour's apartment – luckily for them, for the Russians arrived and searched the Gouzenkos' apartment.

INTREPID STEPS IN

Among famous people involved in the defection episode was Sir William Stephenson (code-named Intrepid), the controversial and famous Winnipegger reportedly sent by Churchill[9] from Britain to New York during the war to establish the British Security Co-ordination. BSC represented several British security and intelligence agencies, including M.I.5 (the domestic security agency); M.I.6 (also known as SIS, the secret intelligence service); and the Special Operations Executive, or SOE. Stephenson had also helped set up the OSS, a precursor to the Central Intelligence Agency (CIA) in the United States.

Truman had dissolved the wartime Office of Secret Services on September 20, 1945. The CIA was not established until two years later. Stephenson's chief concern was the survival of his creation, the BSC, after the war, or at least until a central co-ordinating security agency was formed in North America. The Gouzenko case gave him an excuse to continue BSC.

By coincidence, Stephenson happened to be temporarily in the Ottawa area. Accounts differ as to who called whom, but Norman Robertson, undersecretary of state for External Affairs, alerted Stephenson about the defection. Intrepid, who intensely distrusted the Soviets, barged into the case. From a park across the street from the Gouzenkos' apartment house, he watched Russian embassy people being escorted by police from the apartment, and then called Robertson and convinced him to arrange official protection for the Gouzenkos. In the NFB/CBC documentary *The Most Dangerous Spy*,[10] the narrator quips about agents watching agents in the park, who were watching Gouzenko who was watching them back. It was truly the stuff of spy novels.

At first Gouzenko was concealed in various safe houses in the Ottawa area. Then someone thought of hiding him in Camp X, a secret camp located on the shores of Lake Ontario between Oshawa and Whitby. (One report claims it was Intrepid himself who drove the Gouzenko family to Camp X in the dead of night, but others disagree.[11]) The camp had been established by BSC to train secret agents during the war, and it was also a vital wartime communications centre involved in decoding and transmitting secret messages. An old farmhouse at the camp was one of many hiding places in which the Gouzenkos were sheltered.

Before the Gouzenko case, Canadians still admired the Russians' formidable courage during the long and bloody siege by Germany against the Soviet army on the frozen eastern front. Many Ottawa citizens were captivated by the dashing diplomats at the newly established Russian embassy, and people enticed by the promise of socialism joined the Canadian-Soviet Friendship League.

AN INTERNATIONAL CRISIS

King feared an international uproar over alleged spying activities might spark another world war if Stalin were provoked. After talking to Stephenson, he advised caution and co-operation among the western Allies. King, American president Truman, and British Prime Minister Attlee went into a huddle to decide what to do. Truman was not especially alarmed, believing that the secrets of the atomic bomb would inevitably be revealed in the coming years anyway.[12] He pushed for the arrest of Dr. Alan Nunn May, the atomic scientist implicated in the spy case who had just arrived in Britain from Canada. On October 6, 1945, Mackenzie King directed that a secret order-in-council be passed under the provisions of the War Measures Act, authorizing the RCMP to arrest the suspected spies.

Stephenson, Herbert Hoover of the FBI, and Ernst Cuneo, who had been a top Roosevelt advisor, met to discuss the matter. Some believe it was they who cooked up the idea of leaking the stunning secret through American radio personality Drew Pearson. Pearson's broadcast on February 4, 1946, revealed the sensational spy scandal and nudged Mackenzie King into informing his cabinet. The following day, King ordered a Royal Commission on Espionage to investigate. On February 13, Gouzenko began testifying before the commission, fingering fifteen people for acts he thought were unpatriotic to Canada.

SUSPECTS ROUNDED UP

In an early-morning raid on February 15, 1946, the RCMP rounded up the suspected agents so far named in the Gouzenko hearings. Among those plucked from their beds and locked up were Kathleen Mary Willsher, deputy registrar of the British High Commissioner's Office and a graduate of the London School of Economics; Captain Gordon Lunan of the Canadian Information Service; Edward (Ned)

Mazerall, National Research Council electrical engineer, and Emma Woikin.

The prisoners were confined in barracks at Rockcliffe, where for weeks they were not allowed to speak to each other or anyone outside; each thought he or she was the only one arrested. They were interrogated and bullied. Kay Willsher was reportedly told she could be shot by firing squad for her crime. Lights in the barracks burned twenty-four hours a day. The windows were nailed shut.

Fred Rose, MP, the first communist to be elected to the House of Commons, was arrested later. Dr. Alan Nunn May, an atomic physicist who worked for the National Research Council, was permitted to go to England but was shadowed and later arrested and jailed. He confessed to giving the Russians a sample of uranium for atomic research, saying he thought they had a right to the research denied by their fellow Allies.[13] Another suspect was later arrested in the United States, where he had fled. Eventually there were twenty-six suspects implicated in the case.

On March 2, 1946, Mackenzie King received an advance copy of the first interim report of the royal commission. The news was staggering, and when it was released international events heated up. On March 4 Churchill delivered his explosive Iron Curtain speech warning of Russian aggression, and the Russians angrily replied that he was inciting a new war.[14] In the United States, as early as 1938 the House of Representatives Committee on Un-American Activities had been prying into the lives of people they thought might be engaging in unpatriotic behaviour, focusing on those with pro-communist leanings; now it was becoming a witch-hunt.

On March 6 Alan Nunn May was arrested in Britain, and on March 14 the second interim report was released, implicating MP Fred Rose and the man who had fled to the United States, Sam Carr. The report created political bedlam, especially the news of the arrest of Rose.

Information obtained from detainees by the royal commission was later used against them in trials that followed. *After* the detainees had already testified before the royal commission, they were offered legal counsel, which Emma Woikin at first turned down, probably to save her family costly legal expenses. Others took advantage of this right. Mackenzie King felt uneasy about these ruthless measures, knowing he would be criticized for undemocratic tactics more typical of the Soviet system they condemned.

The first four to be publicly named were Captain Lunan, Edward Mazerall, Kathleen Willsher, and Emma Woikin. Biographer Callwood suggests that these four were chosen because they seemed the most vulnerable.

KINGSTON PEN

On March 13, Magistrate Glen Strike announced that bail would be set for the original four.[15] Emma's brother arrived in Ottawa from Blaine Lake with bail money.

The case was splashed on front pages of newspapers across Canada. Unaware of the local connection, on March 4 and 5 the Saskatoon paper took no particular notice. Suddenly on March 6, 1946, an enormous portrait of her was emblazoned on page 1 of the paper, announcing Mrs. Emma "Voykin" of Hispania (they meant Ospennia), near Blaine Lake, had pleaded guilty to a charge of conspiring to provide secret and confidential information to the USSR. It recounted the tragedies in her life and noted her academic gifts.

On March 16, 1946, her photo accompanied an article entitled "Spy Ring Folk Unassuming" in the Montreal *Standard*. She was pictured again in the *StarPhoenix* with her lawyer and her brother after a court appearance in Ottawa.[16]

The section of the so-called Gouzenko transcripts recording Emma's testimony before the royal commission contains ominous phrases echoed in the McCarthy hearings, which began probing the Hollywood film industry in 1947 to expose suspected communists. During the royal commission hearings, the detainees were grilled about each other. Mr. Fauteux, one of the Supreme Court justices leading the investigations, asked Woikin, "Are you a member of the Communist party?" She answered no. "Were you ever a member of the Communist party?" Again she replied no. Then she was asked if she ever applied to be a member of the party, and if she ever had any dealings with it. To both questions she answered in the negative.

As Mackenzie King noted,[17] the defendants seemed to have been stirred not by offers of money but by idealism, a belief that social justice was superior in the Soviet Union. Canadian delegations to the Soviet Union did not see the starvation and atrocities under the Stalinist regime that are now well known.

After the grim facts of their imprisonment and interrogation came to light in the series of interim reports in March, suspension of the detainees' civil liberties became a hot public issue. John Diefenbaker, in particular, stormed at length in the House of Commons, comparing the case with the reviled Star Chamber[18] and Canada to a police state. M. J. Coldwell and Tommy Douglas of the CCF raised critical questions. When Coldwell said he had just been asked in St. Louis if this was a witch hunt, King assured him they had proof of the detainees' complicity.[19]

On the advice of her lawyer, who had no courtroom experience, Woikin pleaded guilty. In mid-Apri 1946, she was sentenced to two and a half years in prison (plus additional time imposed later for contempt charges). Only Woikin and Kay Willsher pleaded guilty. Questioned later, most of the men dug in their heels. Fred Rose managed to escape testifying at all. Some refused to co-operate as witnesses in trials of the other defendants. Woikin herself at one point answered, "I don't want to answer any more questions," and was cited for contempt of court and sentenced to six months on this charge. Lunan, Gerson, Nightingale, and Adams were also cited for contempt and sentenced to three months. Ten of the defendants went to prison, including May, who was tried in Britain, and Sam Carr.

Those defendants who balked at giving information in the first interrogations, had defenders on the outside, or could afford pricey lawyers either won their court cases or were acquitted on appeal.[20] The sentences of those who remained in Canada varied from three years to Halperin's six. The two women both got three years.

The shadowy world of espionage later popularized by Ian Fleming's James Bond novels and films was a fairly new phenomenon in Canada.[21] The spy scandals cast a glamorous aura over furtive secret agents and snooping undercover informants. Even in the small prairie city of Saskatoon, 282 students signed a document in March 1946 denying the existence of "spy cells" at the University of Saskatchewan.[22]

Perhaps Woikin and the others were lucky their case occurred in Canada. In the infamous Rosenberg case in the United States, Julius and Ethel Rosenberg, who were charged not with treason but with conspiracy, were executed. Earlier, four men and a woman in Marseilles, France, were sentenced to death for espionage.[23] Even in Canada, long before the Gouzenko case, there had been demands for the death penalty for spies. Back in June 1940, Liberal MP Arthur Slaght had risen in the House to demand that spies, saboteurs, and traitors in Canada face the hangman's noose.[24]

The supreme irony is that a real Soviet agent involved in developing the atomic bomb as part of the Manhattan Project in the United States *did* reveal atomic secrets. Although the American government knew about his role, Ted Hall ("The Youngest Spy") was never prosecuted and served no prison sentence.[25]

Woikin served over two years in Kingston Penitentiary. She was a model prisoner, quiet and acquiescent. She wrote profuse, loving letters to her family, and spent long hours painting dark turbulent canvases in oil. She was a "meek and mild little thing," her nephew Fred Konkin recalls, and in prison she was vulnerable to abuse and unwelcome advances. Fortunately one woman became her protector in that sinister setting.

Life After Prison

When she emerged from prison on August 28, 1948, at the age of twenty-seven, Woikin bolted home to the family fold at Blaine Lake. Although her family's reactions had ranged from grief to shame, all the same they were supportive through her ordeal. Her nephew Fred still blames the federal civil service that placed her in such a sensitive position despite her Russian background. He also thinks she was victimized by the Russians.

Even with her family she clammed up about her prison experiences, but she did admit she had seen unspeakable things. When the

StarPhoenix interviewed her at Blaine Lake on December 8, 1948, she said little, but the paper published two of her paintings.

That same month, Richard Nixon announced new evidence had been uncovered by the House Committee on Un-American Activities, "expected to provide the long-sought missing link between the Canadian atom espionage ring and Red agents in the United States."[26]

Emma Woikin moved to Saskatoon after landing a job at a drugstore in January 1949, working for a kindly Jew who didn't care if people called her a spy. On March 5, 1949, she married Lucas (Louie) Sawula, who, relatives say, offered the security she needed.[27] After her drugstore job, she worked for many years for the prestigious law firm of Kyle, Ferguson and Hnatyshyn. The late former Governor-General Ray Hnatyshyn was the son of John Hnatyshyn, an original partner in that firm. Ray told Callwood that Woikin was a prized legal secretary. According to Fred Konkin, Woikin next worked for Peter Makaroff, the first Doukhobor lawyer in Canada. Later she worked at Marcel Cuelenaere's law firm.

Callwood discovered there were several high profile people in Woikin's life: there was a family connection with eminent historian Hilda Neatby. Prime Minister John Diefenbaker helped Emma get a lawyer in Ottawa. Her father's second wife was Natasha, mother of the wife of Dr. J.W.T. Spinks, later president of the University of Saskatchewan.

A SECOND MARRIAGE

Emma and Louie Sawula's first house was a modest wartime dwelling at 1709 Victoria Avenue. Later Emma and Louie bought a bungalow at 425 Avenue G South. With no young children to occupy their attention, the couple led a merry social life, with much carousing and card-playing. It appeared that Emma had bounced back, but after a trip to Russia in 1969, she began drinking heavily. Fred thinks it was because she was crushed by what she learned in Stalinist Russia. "They fed her good, treated her nice," he said, but when she returned to Canada she didn't want to talk about it. She told her family, "When you get there

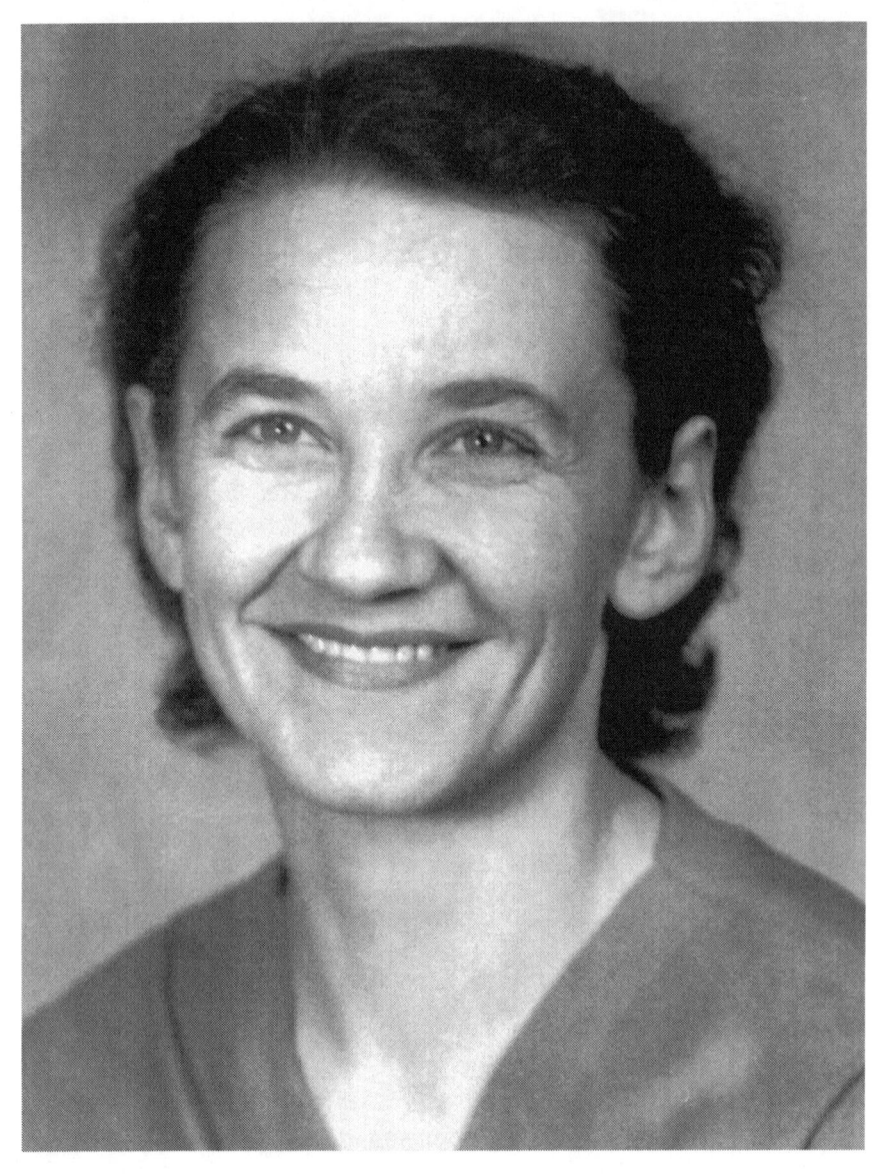

Emma Konkin Woikin of Blaine Lake and Saskatoon. ca. 1955 – *Photo PH 98-113-1, from collection of Fred and Doreen Konkin, courtesy of Saskatoon Public Library Local History Room.*

and see for yourself, it's not true."[28] Emma died on May 22, 1974, of alcohol-related causes.

As for Gouzenko, John Sawatsky's book *Gouzenko: the Untold Story* pieces together the opinions of many who knew him, including several

RCMP officers assigned to guard him. Most heaped scorn on Gouzenko. After the spy scandal, Gouzenko devoted himself to amassing riches to enable a life of comfort and to indulge his appetite for fine food. At first regarded as a hero, he continued for decades to exploit his notoriety, writing books and suing anyone who spoke ill of him. Although Gouzenko made a financial killing from the sensational case, he spent the rest of his days in terror, fearing assassination by the Russians. He died in 1982 in his early sixties.

For those fingered by Gouzenko, the long-term effects were just as distressing. The assault on their reputations ruined their careers. As for the Russian spymaster Zabotin, it is believed he was liquidated for his role in the whole fiasco and arrived home in a coffin.[29]

Detailed evidence from the royal commission report was not disclosed to the public until 1981, so the extraordinary story of Emma Woikin had faded to almost a footnote in Saskatchewan history. But her own words as disclosed in the transcripts provided keen insights into her psyche. In 1984 Canadian author and journalist June Callwood published a sensitive biography, *Emma: the True Story of Canada's Unlikely Spy*. She cast a searchlight over the injustice of a system in which Woikin was denied basic civil rights in place since the Magna Carta[30] and in which defendants in the case with expensive lawyers got off scot-free.

While few would disagree about the impact of the Gouzenko case on East-West relations and the resulting Cold War, historians still disagree whether those charged were guilty of anything serious, and about the justice of provisions of the War Measures Act that violated their civil rights.

Richard St. Barbe Baker donned Arab headgear in Palestine to publicize a lecture tour in 1929. – *Photo by Howard Coster, courtesy of University of Saskatchewan Archives, Richard St. Barbe Baker papers, file M/1.*

RICHARD ST. BARBE BAKER
Pioneer Ecologist

Even the Sahara Desert sands couldn't stop the man people called the Man of the Trees. Richard St. Barbe Baker crusaded around the world to save the forests. The love of trees was in his blood. The son of a gospel-spouting nurseryman, Baker had the zeal of an apostle, but his true deity was the forest. His efforts resulted in the planting and protection of an estimated eleven billion trees.

The forest-green suit he sported must have made people smile. In his day, Baker may have seemed an eccentric and a dreamer, but many of his fellows saw him as a visionary and a crusader. Sometimes called "St. Barbe,"[1] he was respected by fellow tree growers, foresters, conservationists, government officials, religious leaders, educators, and even heads of state. Now, as Nature rocks the planet with titanic calamities, the alarms of the tree huggers are ever more widely heeded.

Richard was almost cradled in the woodlands. His birthplace was near the absurdly named New Forest, one of the oldest forests in England. "St. Barbe" was born October 9, 1889, in the village of West End near Southampton in Hampshire, the eldest of five children of John Richard St. Barbe Baker and his first wife, the former Charlotte Purrott. The elder Baker was inclined to religious evangelism, and young Richard soaked it up.

Richard's lifelong obsession with trees began with a kind of spiritual rebirth in the woods at the age of five. As he wandered in a pine forest near his home in Hampshire, the hushed and mystic woods seemed to him Nature's temple. This cosmic epiphany helps explain his attraction to the Baha'i faith later in life, his sense of oneness with Nature, and a belief in a supreme Life Force from which all energy flows. It also drew him to the Aboriginal peoples of the world who shared his reverence for nature.

Canada first beckoned to Richard when he was a child and a granduncle wrote letters praising the romantic frontier life in Ontario. Already infected with wanderlust by his delight in adventure stories, young Richard was thrilled by his relative's tale of felling a bear with a spade.[2] Later, a visiting Canadian at Cambridge University further enchanted him with the frontier mystique of Canada. In mid-speech the speaker ripped off his starched collar and exclaimed that in Canada such "durned things" were not worn. That dramatic spurning of social restraints impressed young Baker.

Later he met Bishop Lloyd, a leader of the Barr Colonists and the man after whom Lloydminster was named; the Barr Colonists had passed through Saskatoon in April 1903. Lloyd urged young Baker to immigrate to Saskatchewan and enroll at Emmanuel College at the new University of Saskatchewan to study religion and cater to the spiritual needs of isolated farm families. Driven by his own devout impulses and quest for adventure, Baker agreed to go. To prepare himself for a rustic life on the Canadian prairies he learned self defence and slept under the stars.

By chance, when he arrived in Saskatchewan in 1909 a Save the Forest convention was taking place in Regina.[3] Perhaps he attended. By 1910 he was living in a shack he built, with an adjoining stable, on the new university campus in Saskatoon. He was one of its first hundred students, enrolling in Emmanuel College for the 1910-11 academic year.[4] While studying divinity he also took in classes in science, history, and political science.[5]

He shared his shack with two students, thus giving rise to someone's claim that he built the first "student residence" on campus. Among his fellow students was John Diefenbaker, a freshman when Baker was a sophomore. Baker helped to pen the University yell, which he proudly printed in his autobiography. He financed his studies by teaching in schools, working in lumber camps, and writing articles on sports for the *Saturday Press* newspaper in Saskatoon.

Befriending local First Nations people who shared his love of horses, Baker traded Hudson Bay blankets for ponies and hay. Those he remembered were probably Sioux who lived on the Moose Woods (Whitecap) reserve south of the city.

Those years on the prairies were Baker's bronco-busting days, he recalled. He preferred the British system of "gentling" horses, but wild prairie mustangs required different taming techniques than pasture-reared British colts. He was once promised a spirited black Montana mustang if he could ride it. Baker claimed he rode the horse twenty-five miles (40 kilometres) that day, and earned his prize. Later the steed proved capable of seventy miles (110 kilometres) a day. Richard needed such a horse. It was common for young theology students to practise their preaching skills on nearby Anglican congregations, but Baker rode horseback long distances to isolated parishes to preach at mission churches.

In 1910 he also toured the prairies and saw them as "a desert in the making." He was appalled at the relentless ploughing of prairie lands and scowled as farmers chopped down and wrenched out the bluffs of trees that stabilized the soil and sheltered it from the wind. Even then, he urged farmers to plant shelter belts, advice that was to prove prophetic in the Dirty Thirties. Years later he told an interviewer:

> If you want to double your supplies of food, then you should devote twenty percent of your farm to trees, to strategically planted shelter belts.... Trees create a micro-climate [and] lift the water table....[6]

Even then there were experimental stations on the prairies where trees were being tested for use in shelter belts. One of them, the Forestry Farm as it is now called, was established just outside Saskatoon in 1913.

Baker might have crossed paths with W. W. Ashley, a respected early citizen in Saskatoon who mailed out seeds by the thousands, from which sprouted the city's stately elms, now threatened by Dutch elm disease.

It was in northern Saskatchewan that Baker first imagined becoming a forester. Working as a lumberjack near Prince Albert, he observed logging practices that needlessly squandered trees. What he saw led to his belief that clear-cutting and replanting should be a last resort, that it was wiser to let the original trees reproduce. Such a process requires selective felling, impossible with large machinery. Years later he fumed that the forest industry was being prostituted to line the pockets of the lumber barons.

In August 1912, Baker applied for a homestead at NW 25-34-6-W3 near Beaver Creek,[7] but he couldn't fulfil the homestead requirements and cancelled his application in 1913. A man always caught up in a whirlwind of activity, it is not surprising he couldn't fit into his schedule the back-breaking labour of clearing land, or perhaps the act of felling trees and ploughing virgin soil distressed him too much.

There is no record of Baker ever having earned a degree at the University of Saskatchewan other than the honorary doctorate he was awarded in his old age. Instead Baker decided to pursue his education at Cambridge, where his ancestors had studied, so he returned to England, probably in 1913.[8] He apparently studied divinity at Ridley College, an Anglican theological seminary located at Cambridge, but he did not graduate from there either. Perhaps his heart was just not in theology. He was devising a different gospel to spread.

OFF TO WAR

With the coming of war in 1914, Baker completed military training with King Edward's Horse, the King's Overseas Dominions Regiment, and volunteered for overseas service as a trooper. In November 1914 he was commissioned as a second lieutenant in the Remount Service of the Royal Field Artillery and posted to Ireland, where he was appointed riding master to train eight hundred young horsemen for the British Expeditionary Force.

Baker then replaced an officer killed in the 1st Divisional Artillery, 115th Battery, 25th Brigade, and was shipped to France. He claimed he was awarded a Military Cross for pinpointing the location of enemy gun positions, but his crusty battery commander had scoffed at wearing badges of honour and had returned the medal to brigade headquarters.

That same commander talked him out of accepting a position as aide de camp to a general he liked. Another fellow, he observed somewhat acidly, took the promotion and later became a brigadier, then a major general – a road not taken. After a leave in Britain, Baker returned to France, posted to the 39th Brigade. Serving now as a gunner, this former divinity student faced a crisis of conscience when he was expected to actually kill people. He finally rationalized his moral doubts by coming to believe that killing a German meant sending him to a better place.

In France he was hit in a barrage of shells that killed twenty-seven of his mates. Corpses were being pulled from the debris and thrown on a cart. When the burial party noticed that this "corpse" was bleeding, he was taken to hospital, where he woke up three days later.

Baker as a young man. – *Photo courtesy of University of Saskatchewan Archives, Richard St. Barbe Baker papers, file M/1.*

On his recovery Baker was sent to Cork, where he was placed in charge of three hundred army clerks. That must have bored him, for he made a remarkable turn for the better and was posted in 1917 to Swaything Remount Depot. In charge of taking eighteen thousand horses and men to France, he said he crossed the English Channel fifty-eight times without mishap. But his life was in peril when his craft struck a mine. Cannily, Baker had kept a horse on deck. As the barge began to sink, he grabbed the mare's mane and "hitchhiked" alongside the animal as it swam to safety.

Baker was next posted to the Remount Depot at Dieppe on the French coast. After a nocturnal delivery of horses to the front, he was wounded when the train in which he was riding was dive-bombed. He returned to Britain to recover, and was invalided out in 1918 with an 80 per cent disability pension.

From Theology to Forestry

Theology now forgotten, on January 29, 1919, Richard embarked on forestry studies at Gonville and Caius College, Cambridge University. He obtained his forestry diploma in 1920. At last he had papers to prove his worth! Baker applied for a posting in Kenya as Assistant Conservator of Forests, but ran into a roadblock relating to his war injuries. While battling this setback he dipped into invention and commerce.

Before 1920 the only portable homes to roam British roads were ungainly horse-drawn gypsy caravans. In America, early travel trailers were miniature houses mounted on axles – not very aerodynamic.

Richard's first venture in movable housing had been a small revolving shelter he built for his mother. In autumn 1918 he learned there were surplus aircraft materials available for sale. Baker fancied using them to build "caravans," as the British say. He mounted small plywood units on airplane undercarriages, using a coated fabric for lightweight roofs. The prototype he built intrigued the press, and he became a celebrity. Shortly he set up a mini-factory called Navarac Caravans, and his pint-sized mobile dwellings were copied by other British firms. Later he was to use them on safaris around the world.[9]

He planned to take his caravan on a European tour via road and river barge. But his plan was halted when, impressed by his drive and blooming good health, the Colonial Office relented in 1920, awarding him the coveted post of assistant conservator of forests in Kenya.

Men of the Trees in Africa

In 1922, despairing at the march of the desert into once-forested lands, Baker coaxed thousands of tribesmen into trying to stop the killing of forests by founding an association called the Men of the Trees. Tribal dances were an age-old tradition in Kenya, and he sparked the interest of tribesmen by promoting the Dance of the Trees, offering prizes for best performance and costume. The organization, which was modelled on the Boy Scouts, required young dancers to perform a good

Baker with Nigerian tribesmen in Benin. – *Photo courtesy of University of Saskatchewan Archives, Richard St. Barbe Baker papers, file M/8.*

deed every day. Their good deed, they were told, could be to plant a certain number of trees each day. Soon newly planted saplings sprang up throughout the land.

In 1924 he exported the Men of the Trees concept to England, and in 1929 to Palestine. Later the movement branched out to more than ninety countries, sometimes under different names. Now it is called the International Tree Foundation.[10] In 1929 he took another Colonial Office assignment in Nigeria, where he focused on the mahogany forests. His principal feat there was to establish those forests on a sustained yield basis. He lost one posting due to "insubordination" when he deflected a blow meant for one of the tribesmen, and was transferred elsewhere in the colony. A severe bout of malaria finally sent him home to England in about 1929. Put on a boat for England, he was not expected to arrive alive, but he did.

Illnesses seem to have brought Baker to the brink of death several times, but malaria is the only ailment named in his books, apart from injuries. His mysterious illnesses mostly involved high and prolonged fevers, symptoms of malaria. He claimed he was nursed back to health by a vegetarian couple. A vegetarian as a child, he later regarded his vegetarianism as a spiritual act in harmony with animals – except for goats. He ranted against the ruin inflicted by goats. Actually, he wasn't fond of *any* animal raised for food because historically animal husbandry had led to the plundering of forests to create grazing lands for domestic herds. (How he would have hated what is happening in Brazil.)

He had amazing powers of recovery, if his memoirs are to be believed. One time after a shipboard injury a doctor insisted that Baker's leg must be lopped off because gangrene had set in. Baker refused, saying a forester needed two legs. Baker won the argument, kept his leg, and survived.

After returning home, he turned his attention to Palestine. In 1929 "St. Barbe" convinced religious leaders there, traditionally at odds, to unite in a plan to restore their desert lands to forest. He didn't categorically oppose logging, but pushed for long-term forest management and selective logging to help the forests sustain themselves.

Baker Becomes an Author

In the summer of 1930 Baker crossed the ocean for a lecture tour of the United States and Canada. Arriving almost penniless in New York, he was promptly courted by a publisher who wanted a book out of him. Needing the money, Baker churned out an entire book in one month, dictating to stenographers until midnight, after which he ate his one meal of the day.

Baker crisscrossed North America consulting foresters about a lofty forestry project he was planning for the United States. He sold Franklin D. Roosevelt (who was not yet president) on the plan, which developed into the Civilian Conservation Corps (CCC) and provided employment to six million men. For years he returned annually to follow up the work of the CCC.[11]

About that time he was invited by the Society of American Foresters to help prepare a forestry plan for them. He met the leader of the Save the Redwoods League in California, and thus began his decades-long campaign to preserve those ancient towering forests. Lowell Thomas, a famous broadcaster who had interviewed him in New York, was an effective ally in that campaign. Thomas dubbed him "Lawrence of Africa" because he had "done for the African people what Lawrence of Arabia did for the Arabs."[12]

Whenever Baker spoke of the redwood forest, this "Temple of the Almighty," his eloquence was spellbinding. Only the redwoods, he said, had survived the Ice Age, and some existing trees were two thousand years old. His evangelical upbringing erupted in such declarations as: "The Sylvan pantheon that God did plan, but builds but once, [is] being desecrated by the demons of destruction."[13]

He was to trek to California eighteen times on that mission, and with his fellows engage in titanic battles with lumber moguls. With public

Civilian Conservation Corps (CCC) forestation crew planting trees in a burned out area. Baker was instrumental in convincing President Roosevelt to institute the forestry plan. – *Photo courtesy of University of Saskatchewan Archives, Richard St. Barbe Baker papers, file M/7.*

support, a National Redwood Forest and a state forest were set aside to preserve the majestic trees. He even provoked Cold War forestry rivalry when the USSR exhorted its citizens to triple the American shelter belt planting record.

In 1946 he married Doreen Whitworth Long of Strensham, Worcestershire. She had been his secretary at the Men of the Trees headquarters in England. The Bakers' daughter, Angela, was born that same year, and a son, Paul, in 1949. But Baker's nomadic activities kept him away from his family for frequent and long periods, and the marriage ended in divorce in 1959.

Baker's greatest challenge was his battle against the deserts, which he saw as armies on the march. To arrest the advance of the Sahara, the world's largest desert, was daunting but not impossible, he thought, because parts of it are fed by underground rivers and basins, creating the miracle of oases.[14] Rescuing the deserts was to be a lifelong battle, never won, but there were small triumphs.

In 1952 he led the first of two Sahara expeditions across thousands of miles of desert carrying out an ecological survey. That safari was described in his 1954 book *Sahara Challenge*. After that, he never tired of preaching about it. "It took about 1,500 years for the Arabs to make the Sahara Desert. In the United States, it [took] only forty-four years to form the Dust Bowl," he said.[15] (Actually the process of desertification in the Saraha is said to have begun eight thousand years ago.[16]) If he were still alive, Baker might compare the size of the Sahara today, more than eight million square kilometres, with its size of five million square kilometres in 1952.

Baker said the way to reclaim large tracts of arid land was to enlist the aid of local people, as he had done in Kenya. His technique for planting trees in sand came, improbably, from an oilman. When an Esso representative suggested using petroleum by-products to anchor the saplings, Baker thought he was a slippery operator with a profit agenda. But soon he was convinced. Nursery-grown saplings, their roots encased no doubt in a ball of rich earth, were planted in clumps and then tankers sprayed a petroleum mulch on the surface. The mulch stabilized the sand and drew up heat, lifting water from beneath the surface, he wrote.

A MAY-DECEMBER MARRIAGE

Ever on the move, in early 1958 he was at Mount Cook, New Zealand, staying with fellow tree-lovers the Burnetts on their sheep ranch. Catriona was the engaging daughter of former MP Thomas David Burnett. After parting from Catriona, Richard Baker realized he was in love. The aging but energetic tree-hugger dashed off a marriage proposal by mail, and Catriona accepted. Despite her ready willingness, he felt compelled to return to Britain for a marathon 550 kilometre horseback tour of Hampshire, Surrey, and Sussex, lecturing at sixty schools along the way. Soon afterwards, while waiting for his two children to complete a 40-kilometre riding tour, Baker joined a gliding club. After days of soaring silently over the forests he was embarrassed to ask pilots to keep towing him, so he joined the Hampshire Air Club and became a fledgling pilot at the age of sixty-nine.

Baker then packed up his possessions and flew to New Zealand via Moscow on a new Russian jet, and was ecstatic when he was permitted to take over the controls briefly.

He married Catriona Burnett on October 7, 1959, in a village 160 kilometres from Mt. Cook.[17] Guests gave trees instead of gifts. It was two days before his seventieth birthday; Catriona was forty-five.

In 1963, at the age of seventy-four, Richard completed another marathon ride, this time to outdo the recent failed attempt of a young Dutchman to ride across New Zealand on horseback. Baker claimed he rode from the northernmost forests of the country to the southernmost, travelling 40 kilometres and lecturing at five schools each day, for a total distance of almost 2,000 kilometres.

In 1964 Baker set out on a second safari around the perimeter of the Sahara. Since decolonization, twenty-five new countries now bordered the desert. He envisioned that if "two million square miles [five million square kilometres] of the world's most famous desert could be made to grow food, it would be virtually adding a new continent to the world."[18] His book *Sahara Conquest* described that perilous trip. At the World Forestry Conference in Madrid in June, Baker gathered African delegates together to discuss an ambitious Sahara reclamation programme.

Baker met world leaders throughout his life. He met President Roosevelt in 1932 and President Johnson just after Kennedy's death in 1963. He met Pope Pius XI in 1926 and convinced him to take the Men of the Trees off his list of banned books (placed there because of its secret handshake and a password – Baker argued it was not a secret society but a brotherhood like the Scouts, which also has a salute and handshake). He worked out a shelter belt programme with Indian Prime Minister Nehru. Baker met Italy's *Il Duce* when Mussolini was a waiter in a London restaurant, and later in Rome. Years later he had an audience with Pope Paul and visits with a cardinal who was the director-general of the Food and Agriculture Organization of the United Nations. The following year at the United Nations the Pope implored world leaders to "reclaim the deserts and feed the people." Baker also squawked at De Gaulle for atomic testing in the Sahara by the French – to no avail.

At ninety, one of Richard's last activist stands was a struggle to save the pine forests of India.

In recognition of his pioneer work in conservation, in 1950 Baker was made an honorary graduate of Biltmore Forestry School in the United States. In 1971 he was awarded an Honorary Doctorate of Laws at the University of Saskatchewan. The presenter was his former classmate, John Diefenbaker. In 1977 Britain named him an Officer of the Order of the British Empire (O.B.E.).

Richard St. Barbe Baker died at the age of ninety-two on June 9, 1982, while on a stopover in Saskatoon. Just days earlier, he had helped to plant a poplar tree near the grave site of John Diefenbaker. His Baha'i faith forbids a journey of more than four hours after death, so he was buried in Saskatoon among the trees at Woodlawn Cemetery, a fittingly named final resting place. Nearby, the tree-lined Memorial Avenue honours Saskatoon's war dead.

Although Baker never set down permanent roots in Saskatchewan, it is appropriate that his final resting place should be the country where he first dreamed of becoming a forester, and where he first recognized the potential for climatic devastation in the clear-cutting of forests and relentless ploughing of agricultural lands. Thus had begun his passionate commitment to conservation.

John Diefenbaker (right) presents an honourary degree to Richard St. Barbe Baker at the University of Saskatchewan fall convocation, 1971. – *Photo courtesy of University of Saskatchewan Archives, Richard St. Barbe Baker papers, file M/6.*

The Richard St. Barbe Baker Foundation was formed in Saskatoon by his admirers during his last years. Baker also left a rich legacy of highly quotable remarks. He was not modest about his achievements, which are recounted in his many books cited in the British *Who's Who*. American newspapers occasionally reviewed his books. Evidently awed by his sincerity and conviction, most reviewers acclaimed him, although some bemoaned his lack of documentation or smiled at his flowery phrases. One felt he was gullible and naïve to believe the statements of diplomats.[19] Another snickered at his writing ability, but thought the book *Africa Drums* was "effective." Baker did sometimes spout gushing

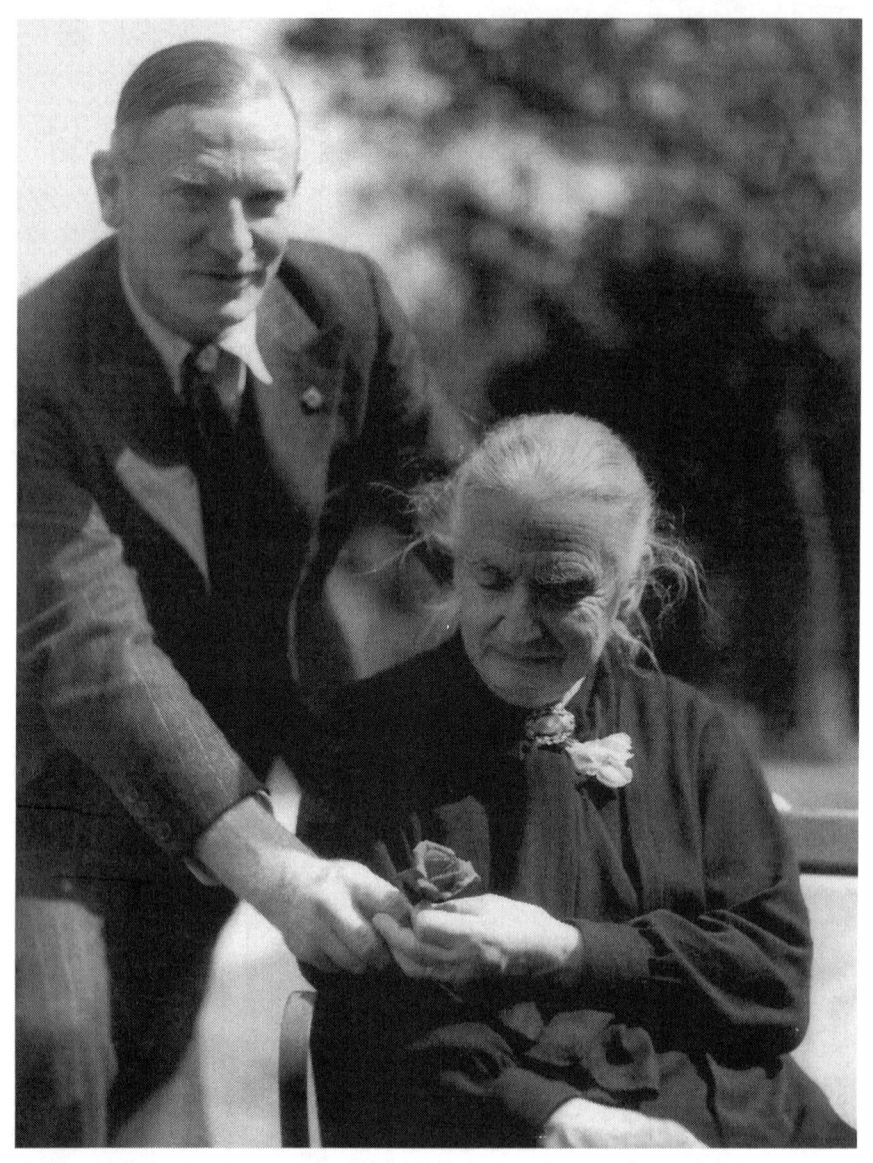

Baker with his mother, probably in England. – *Photo courtesy of University of Saskatchewan Archives, Richard St. Barbe Baker papers, file M/10.*

imagery such as: "Our woods and forests, the indispensable lungs of our earth organism, are falling into a murderous dance of death."[20] Mixed metaphors or not, he swayed millions. On June 9, 1960, he thundered at a PTA group:

Millions of acres of rich farm lands are now deserts as the direct result of wholesale destruction of trees and forests.... Of the earth's 30 billion trees, already nine million acres [are now replaced by] desert.... We submit that if the earth loses a third of its tree cover it will assuredly die. The water table will sink beyond recall, and life on this planet will become impossible. It is a deplorable fact that during the past fifty years we have been skinning the earth alive.[21]

Baker abandoned religion as a career, but he was forever driven by his social conscience. One writer compared his humanitarianism to that of Tolstoy and Gandhi.[22] Tributes abound, testifying to Baker's world-wide impact. The late Viscount Bledisloe, governor general of New Zealand, called Baker "the greatest authority in the English-speaking world on the supreme value of silviculture."[23]

Though Baker failed to restrain the expanding Sahara, his public pleas sowed seeds from which sprouted living forests around the world. And the struggle goes on. Arguably Baker was a prophet, for his warnings about mankind's wilful destruction of the planet are ever more compelling. The words of an anonymous author could have made a fitting epitaph: "His is the voice raised in the wilderness to make the desert blossom again."[24]

ENDNOTES

NOTES TO KATHLEEN RICE

1. J. B. Weichel, "She Paddled Her Own Canoe," Stratford *Beacon-Herald*, undated clipping ca. 1963, from St. Marys Museum, St. Marys, Ontario.
2. *University of Toronto Commencement, Friday June 8th, 1906* (Toronto: The University Press, 1906); University of Toronto Archives, P87-0046 (54).
3. Saskatchewan Archives Board, Inactive Teacher Registers.
4. Saskatchewan Archives Board, Teacher Registers. In Duncan's fictionalized biography, Rice was accompanied to Yorkton by a woman friend who hated the wilds and later returned to civilization.
5. "Eligibility for entry was determined by age, status, gender and naturalization.... In 1876 the sex of the entrant became germane. From this point on women were eligible only if they were the sole head of a family; although in 1919, widows of veterans who could have claimed a right of entry were allowed to make that entry." From Kirk Lambrecht's *The Administration of Dominion Lands, 1870-1930* (Regina: Canadian Plains Research Centre, 1991), 22.
6. On June 7, 1913, Lincoln Rice applied for entry on the bottom half of NW 32-56-26 west of 1st Meridian. On April 24, 1914, he applied for a pre-emption on Part NE-31-56-26. He acquired patent in 1918. Dominion of Canada Crown Lands Registry, Archives of Manitoba, microfilm.
7. Amisk/Beaver Lake website, http://www.quantumlynx.com/ denarebeach/bcity1.htm, and other sources.
8. "Ontario Girl Winning Out as Pioneer and Prospector," [Toronto?] *Star*, Jan. 28, 1928 or 1929, from St. Marys Museum, Ontario; distance calculator in Government of Canada, Dept. of Natural Resources website, Canadian Geographical Names, http://GeoNames2.NRCan.gc.ca.
9. Frederick Griffin, "College Woman Braves a Life in the Wilds," Toronto *Star*, Dec. 21, 1928.
10. Ibid.

11. 3rd Battalion Attestation Papers, Canadian Overseas Expeditionary Force, Soldiers of the First World War, RG 150, accession 1992-93/166, Box 8222-6, National Archives of Canada; from NAC ArchiviaNet website http://www.archives.ca/02/0201_e.html.
12. Duncan says they met in 1912. Archival records show Rice was teaching in Yorkton that year, and for part of 1913 was occupied with clearing the bush on her homestead near The Pas.
13. For example, she unearthed an old diary by an unknown trapper and inserted fragments of it attributed to Woosey. No University of Toronto records verify that she won a gold medal. The homesteading venture with her brother is not mentioned. Newspaper accounts say she taught at several more places than those mentioned in the book. Kathleen's whitewater canoe trek down the Sturgeon-Weir River rapids was in 1928, not before she moved in with Woosey in 1914. Her tragic last days are omitted.
14. Helen Duncan, *Kate Rice: Prospector* (Toronto: Simon & Pierre, 1984), 10.
15. Bessie G. Ferguson, "First Woman Prospector 'Swings on Her Own Gate'," Toronto *Mail*, Dec. 20, [1924?].
16. "St. Mary's [sic] Girl Prospects in the Lonely Wilds of Northern Manitoba," Toronto *Globe,* Jan. 14, 1928; John Crozier, "This Woman Lives Dangerously," World Digest, June 1939 .
17. According to the Snow Lake website www.snowlake.com, he found gold in 1913, but the *Saga of Snow Lake* indicates gold was first discovered in the area by Jack Nutt in 1916.
18. "Toronto Woman Grad is Now Prospecting," Toronto *Star,* Feb. 12 or 13, 1934.
19. Kathleen Rice, "Woman Prospector Travels Alone Through Manitoba Wilds," *Star Weekly,* Oct. 5, 1929.
20. Laurel Archer, *Northern Saskatchewan Canoe Trips* (Eric, Ont.: Boston Mills Press, 2003), 31.
21. Correspondence, Sam Waller Museum, The Pas.
22. Kathleen Rice, "The Aurora-Arctic Will O' the Wisp," *Journal of the Royal Astronomical Society of Canada* 26, no. 7 (1932), 304-12.
23. "Map Showing Commercial Development in Manitoba and part of Saskatchewan," published by the federal Dept. of the Interior, 1929, and reprinted in *Manitoba Historical Atlas* (Winnipeg: Historical and Scientific Society of Manitoba, 1970).
24. Duncan, *Kate Rice: Prospector,* author's note, 13.
25. Letter to Mr. Fennell, Feb. 9, 1943, University of Toronto Archives.
26. Donald Jones, "Of a Tarnished Golden Rainbow," Toronto *Star,* Nov., 1985.

Sources Not Cited in Endnotes

"College Girl Prospector." Toronto *Telegram,* July 18, 1928.
Correspondence and photos, University of Toronto Archives.

Correspondence and photos, St. Marys Museum, St. Marys, Ontario.
"Girl Braves North's Trails," Toronto *Star*, Dec. 20, 1928.
"Girl Digs at End of Rainbow, Uncovers Pot of Gold," Toronto *Mail*, Aug. 4, 1928.
Herb Lake website, http://www3.telus.net/HerbLake/index.htm.
History of Wekusko Lake website, http://www.jhk.mb.ca/wekusko/ history. No longer active.
"Lives in Northern Bush Because She Prefers It." Toronto *Daily Star*, Dec. 21, 1928.
Snow Lake Salute to the Trail Blazers [pamphlet], Snow Lake, Manitoba 1967.
"Woman Makes Lucky Mineral Find, the First to Do So in North Manitoba." Toronto *Mail*, July 16, 1928.

NOTES TO WILL JAMES

1. Given such a legal quagmire, the estate finally went to his younger brother Auguste Dufault, an outcome that was probably what James intended.
2. Books and magazine articles say her name was Josephine, but in the NFB film *Alias Will James* (directed by Jacques Godbout, National Film Board of Canada, 1988) a close-up of the record of his birth in the parish register shows her name as Flor Pauline.
3. Two 1911 photographs at the Glenbow Archives showing him beside his sod shack note that he was working on the Moir Ranch, according to the donor, a member of the Moir family who took over James's homestead land. But most American books that show one of these photographs claim it was taken at the Sage Creek Line Camp in Alberta, where he may have also worked.
4. Greg Stott, "Wanted: Will James," *Equinox*, March/April 1995, 54-65.
5. *Atlas of Saskatchewan: Celebrating the Millennium* (Saskatoon: University of Saskatchewan, 1999), 64.
6. Laurier Gareau, "Ernest Dufault, alias Will James," *Revue Historique* 2, no. 4 (May 1992): 11.
7. *Val Echo [Val-echo]: a History of Val Marie*, compiled by teachers and pupils of Val Marie High School, mimeographed (Val Marie: Val Echo, 1955), 14.
8. There are two files under the name of William R. James: (1) SW-25-2-12-W3 (file no. 2444664); James applied for entry on this quarter on July 12, 1911; (2) NW-25-2-12-W3 (file no. 2446668), June 23, 1911. Homestead records, Saskatchewan Archives Board.
9. *Wagon Trails Along the White Mud* (Val Marie, Sask.: Val Marie Homemakers Club [Women's Institutes], n.d.), 98.
10. *Val-Echo*, 98.
11. "Il semble que la jeune Dufault ait eu maille àpartir avec la Police montée canadienne, pour une histoire de bagarre dans une saloon de Calgary. Accusé de meurtre, il s'enfuit au Montana." From preface by Jacques Godbout in *Will James, L'enfance d'un cow-boy solitaire* (Montreal, Quebec: Editions du

Boreal, 1989), 8.
12. Bramlett, *Ride for the High Points*, 49-50.
13. Will James, *Lone Cowboy: My Life Story* (New York: Charles Scribner & Sons, 1926), 359.
14. Will James, *Smoky the Cowhorse* (New York: Scribner's, 1926, 1932).
15. Stott, "Wanted: Will James," 36.
16. Bramlett, *Ride for the High Points*, 128.
17. William Gardner Bell, *Will James: the Life and Works of a Lone Cowboy* (Flagstaff, Ariz.: Northland Press, 1987), 101.
18. Anthony Amaral, *Will James. The Gilt-Edged Cowboy* (Los Angeles: Westernlore Press, 1967), 172.
19. Alan Jensen, "The Legend of Will James and the True Story Behind It," *Legacy*, February-April, 1998, 19.

Sources Not Cited in Endnotes

Jensen, Allan. "Will James: Legacy of the Open Range." Unpublished manuscript.

Neil, J. M., ed. *Will James: the Spirit of the Cowboy*. Casper, Wyoming: Nicolaysen Art Museum/University of Nebraska Press, 1985.

NOTES TO CHARLIE PARMER

1. Grant MacEwan, *Poking Into Politics* (Edmonton: Institute of Applied Art Limited, 1966).
2. "Gun-Toter of Old West Who Was Turned Down by Jesse James, Worked for Two Years for Buffalo Bill, Lives Near Dundurn," Saskatoon *StarPhoenix*, Sept. 26, 1932.
3. Harvey Mawson, Dundurn, correspondence, Nov. 2003.
4. Theresa Heukert, "Dundurn's Outlaw Farmer," *Western People*, May 30, 1966.
5. Richard Brownlee, *Grey Ghosts of the Confederacy: Guerrilla Warfare in the West, 1861-1865* (Baton Rouge: Louisiana State University Press, 1984, reprint of 1958 ed.); "Missouri Partisan Roster of Known Members of Quantrill Gang," The Missouri Partisan Ranger website, http://www.rulen.com/partisan/roster.htm.
6. "The James Gang Women," Jesse James website, http://rosecity.net/trains/james_gang_women.html.
7. Harvey Mawson, ed., *Fast Gun: the Life and Times of Charles Augustus Parmer, Dundurn's Legendary Gunman* (Dundurn: Dundurn Historical Society, 1998).
8. "Gun-Toter of Old West...," Saskatoon *StarPhoenix*, Sept. 26, 1932.
9. Barb Glen, "Finding the Man History Forgot," Saskatoon *Sun*, May 17, 1992, p. 3.
10. Mawson, *Fast Gun*, 47.
11. Saskatchewan Archives Board, Canada Department of the Interior Home-

stead Records, File No. 12499554 for Charles Parmer (NW-4-34-4-W3).
12. "Gun-Toter of Old West...."
13. Mawson, *Fast Gun*, 45.
14. Ibid., 43.
15. "Associate of Notorious Jesse James, Man Who Boasted Two Notches on Gun, Charles A. Parmer Dies Near Dundurn," Saskatoon *StarPhoenix*, Dec. 28, 1935.
16. Tara De Ryk, "Marker to Immortalize Dundurn Legend," Davidson *Leader*, July 5, 1999.

NOTES TO TOM HOURIE

1. Ronald Kell, *The Postal History of the District of Assinboia 1882-1905* (Toronto: The Unitrade Press, 1987).
2. Orkneymen were valued for their honesty, physical stamina, and dexterity at paddling. A 1750 account by Murdoch Mackenzie described them as "healthy, hardy, well-shaped, subject to few diseases, and capable of an abstemious and industrial life." Nor were they clannish or violent like their Highland cousins.
3. The book *Metis Families: A Genealogical Compendium* (Pawtucket, RI: Quintin Publications, 1996), probably based on extensive Métis scrip records held by the National Archives, lists fourteen: Margaret, Tom, Alexander, Edwin James, Albert Edward, Peter, Elizabeth Ann, Flora, Lydia, Samuel, Marie, Joseph, Henry (probably Harry), and Philip. Peter and his family came by ox-cart to Prince Albert in the early 1870s. The year after the Resistance they moved to Regina, where they were living at the time of Tom's death.
4. In one version of this story they proceeded to Qu'Appelle; in another they remained at Broadview, which were in any event fairly close.
5. NWMP Commissioner Acheson Grosford Irvine was usually called Colonel. As a quasi-military force, the Mounties were often accorded military titles that differed from their actual NWMP rank.
6. "Peter Hourie Reminiscences," c. 1910, Saskatchewan Archives Board, R-E 3023.
7. *Map Shewing Mounted Police Stations & Patrols throughout the North-West territories during the year 1889* ([Ottawa]: Dominion of Canada, [1889?]).
8. John Hawkes, *The Story of Saskatchewan and Its People*, vol. 1 (Chicago: Clarke, 1924), 258.
9. *The Riel Rebellion 1885* (Montreal: Witness Publishing House, [1885]); cover title: Riel Rebellion Reports; written on library copy: July 21, 1885, and November 16, 1885 by two different hands.
10. Peter Hourie did not have a son named Frank.
11. Clarke's Crossing [a.k.a. Clark's Crossing] was 130 kilometres (80 miles) from Prince Albert, much more than the 26 kilometres (16 miles) Hourie suppos-

edly sprinted to the city after his swim. Furthermore, being to the west, it was far out of his way. Source: table of distances in T. Arnold Haultain's *Souvenir Number of the Illustrated War News,* Saturday, July 4, 1885, p. 8.

12. Writers and historians have debated the correct terms for English-speaking people of partial Aboriginal descent. "Mixed descent" is imprecise as to ethnic origin, "Métis" suggests French ancestry, and "country-born" merely suggests Canadian birth. Some still call the children of English-speaking fathers and Aboriginal mothers "half-breeds," but it has a pejorative ring. The term English or Scots Métis has been used in this text.

13. The government telegraph lines had reached Battleford in 1883 and Duck Lake in 1884. By early 1885 the lines ran from Qu'Appelle through Touchwood and Clarke's Crossing to Battleford and Edmonton, with a branch from Clarke's Crossing to Prince Albert. But the lines between Prince Albert, Clarke's Crossing, and Humboldt were cut. The government scrambled to restore those vital lines. By March 28 the line to Battleford had been repaired but not the one to Prince Albert. *Saskatchewan Herald,* Mar. 27, 1885, p. 1; Apr. 23, 1885, p. 2.

14. C. R. Mayson, "Tom Hourie," parts 1-3, broadcast on Prince Albert radio station CKBI, October [19?], November 6 and 20, 1953. Copies held at Saskatchewan Archives, R-73.III.2.f.

15. See *Saskatchewan Historical Trails,* Canada Surveys and Mapping Branch, 1963. Another ferry in the area called the Hudson Bay Crossing was also known as the McLeod Crossing. There were several other ferry sites at which he might have crossed, but the Fenton ferry route seems most likely.

16. From 1900 to 1942, the ice broke up only four times before April 1, but in 1930 it broke up as early as March 11. "42-Year Record of River Ice Break-Up Here," Saskatoon *StarPhoenix,* n.d., from Saskatoon Public Library Local History files.

17. Upriver in nearby Saskatoon, the annual spectacle of the ice breakup attracted crowds to the riverbanks to watch the spectacular event, until the Gardiner Dam was built in the 1960s. Observers watched colossal chunks as big as a house heaving and crashing in the river. For several years in a row the ice knocked out the city's wooden railway bridge, first built in 1889, until cement piers were installed.

18. Professor Gordon Giesbrecht, thermal physiologist, University of Manitoba, on CBC Radio, "Sounds Like Canada," Nov. 2002.

19. Gordon Giesbrecht, email correspondence, Nov. 17, 2003.

20. *The Book of the American West* (New York: Bonanza Books, 1964), 6.

21. *Saskatoon StarPhoenix,* July 15, 1926, p. 31.

22. June Callwood, *Emma: the True Story of Canada's Unlikely Spy* (Toronto: Stoddart Publishing, 1984), 14

23. Copy of Official Diary of Lieut. Col. [Acheson Gosford] Irvine, [s.l.], Canadian Institute for Historic Microreproduction, 1985, CHIM microfilm number 30572.

24. William Francis Butler, *The Great Lone Land: a Narrative of Travel and Adventure in the North-West of America* (Edmonton: M.G. Hurtig Ltd., 1968; first published by Musson, 1924).
25. Sir Fred Middleton, *Suppression of the Rebellion in the North West Territories of Canada 1885* (Toronto: University of Toronto, 1948), 14.
26. Diary of Lieut. Col. Irvine.
27. Joseph Kinsey Howard, Strange Empire: *A Narrative of the Northwest* (Westport, Conn.: Greenwood Press, 1974, first published 1952), 425.
28. *The Riel Rebellion* (Regina *Daily Star*, [1935]), 6.
29. T. Arnold Haultain, *Canadian Pictorial & Illustrated War News*, pt. 2, Aug. 29, 1885, 3.
30. Hawkes, *The Story of Saskatchewan*, 258.
31. *The Riel Rebellion*, 11.
32. "William Diehl, 82, Helped Take Riel: Carried First News of Arrest," single typescript page, affidavit, 30 Sept. 1919, Manitoba Archives, MG3 C16 Diehl, William.
33. Charlotte Gordon, "Mr. Robert Armstrong – the Captor of Louis Riel," *Western Home Monthly*, May 1923, p. 16.
34. "Funeral Tomorrow," newspaper clipping [from Dawson City?], Dec. 4, 1908, Yukon Archives.
35. Canada, Department of the Interior, RG 15, D-11-3 vol. 192, File HB 1640.
36. Homestead Records, Saskatchewan Archives Board, File # 323993.
37. Andrew Knox, "Prince Albert and Politics" (address), Dec. 18, 1936, from Prince Albert Historical Museum.
38. "The Gallantry of Tom Hourie," Regina *Leader*, [1971?], from Saskatchewan Archives Board.
39. Pierre Berton, *Klondike* (Toronto: Penguin Books, 1990; first published 1958, rev. 1972) 119.
40. "Their Weight in Gold: Flour and Dogs are Now in Strong Demand at Rich Klondyke," Victoria *Daily Colonist*, July 7, 1897, p. 5.
41. "Undreamt Of Wealth: Mail Carrier Reports That the Klondyke Country Richer Than at First Supposed – Will Be a Producer of Millions," Victoria *Daily Colonist*, Sunday, July 11, 1897, p. 6.
42. *Saskatchewan Times* (Prince Albert), Sept. 14, 1897.
43. Regina *Leader*, Aug. 26, 1897.
44. Hourie's name does not appear in the comprehensive lists compiled by the NWMP starting in early 1898 when posts were set up at the Canadian border, suggesting he probably did arrive in 1897 as stated in his death notice.
45. Trudy Duivenvoorden, "Camels in the Cariboo," *The Beaver* 76, no. 1 (Feb./March 1996): 30-34.
46. Regina *Leader*, July 27, 1897, p. 1
47. Letter from B. R. Shaw, written at Dawson City, June 15 [1897], to O. A. Schade of Seattle, published in Victoria *Daily Colonist*, July 22, 1897, p. 2.

48. Regina *Leader,* Aug. 19, 1897, p. 1.
49. Food for the Yukon: Five Head of Cattle Turned into Pemmican," Regina *Leader,* Aug. 19, 1897, p. 1; "Town and Country," Regina *Leader,* Sept. 9, 1897.
50. Berton, *Klondike,* 472.
51. Schedule A: Application for Grant for Placer Mining and Affidavit of Applicant No. 12670, Yukon Archives.
52. Andrew Knox, "Prince Albert and Politics," unpublished typescript read at a meeting Dec. 18, 1936.
53. "Death Records from Green's Mortuary," http://www.yukongenealogy.com/content/database_funerals.htm; "Funeral Tomorrow," newspaper account, [Dawson City?], Dec. 4, 1908, from Yukon Archives.
54. "Address of sympathy from Yukon on the death of Tom Hourie," unpublished typescript, Yukon Archives.
55. "Peter Hourie, Reminiscences."

Sources Not Cited in Endnotes

Beal, Bob and Rod Macleod. *Prairie Fire: the 1885 North-West Rebellion.* Toronto: McClelland & Stewart, 1984.
Berton, Laura Beatrice. *I Married the Klondike.* Toronto: McClelland & Stewart, 1961.
Canada. Sessional Papers, NWMP, 8a, 1899. "Return of Casual Cases Tried and Prisoners Confined at Battleford NWT, During Year Ended November 1885."
Cummins Rural Directory Maps. Series. Winnipeg: Cummins Map Co., [1920].
Friesen, Victor Carl. *Where the River Runs.* Calgary: Fifth House, 2001.
General Map of the Northwest Territories and of the Province of Manitoba, rec. and corrected to 31st August 1894. ([Ottawa]: Minister of the Interior).
Jefferson, Robert. *Fifty Years on the Saskatchewan.* Canadian North-West Historical Society Publications 1, no. v. Battleford: 1929.
Macdonald, C. *The Dominion Telegraph.* Battleford: Canadian North-West Society Publications, 1930.
Satterfield, Archie. *Chilkoot Pass Then and Now.* Alaska Northwest Publishing Co., 1973.
Schilling, Rita. *Gabriel's Children.* North Battleford: Turner Warwick, 1983.
Steele, Samuel Benfield. *Forty Years in Canada.* Toronto: McGraw-Hill Ryerson, 1972; first published in London, 1915.
"Tom Hourie Swam River at Break-Up," n.p., n.d. (probably *StarPhoenix*), scrapbook 1, p. 78, Saskatoon Public Library Local History Room.
Wallace, Jim. *Forty-Mile to Bonanza: the North-West Mounted Police in the Klondike Gold Rush.* (Calgary: Bunker-to-Bunker Publishing, 2000.
The Western Canadians 1600-1900. Vol. 1. Toronto: Genealogical Research Library, 1994.

NOTES TO NORMAN FALKNER

1. Census of Canada, 1901, Saskatoon West, Reel T-6554.
2. Mrs. A. E. Nurse, letter to City Council, Jan. 18, 1960, recommending that a city street be named after C. T. Falkner.
3. "Death Claims City Treas. C. T. Falkner: Succumbs After a Month's Illness," [ill.] Saskatoon *Phoenix*, Feb. 21, 1908.
4. The Auditorium Roller Rink, located beside a curling rink (probably temporary) near the riverbank in a 1911 fire insurance map by Charles E. Goad, appears as an enclosed structure with a rounded roof in early photographs. It was evidently used for ice skating in winter. The report of a fire mentioning the rink as "the place where the R Jays and the Civics did battle" suggests it was also used as a hockey arena. "Many Citizens Visit Fire Scene," Saskatoon *Phoenix*, May 11, 1914.
5. A photo of the C. T. Falkner house was published in the Saskatoon *Phoenix* Illustrated Supplement, Christmas, 1903, p. 1.
6. "Norman Falkner, A One-Legged Figure Skater: Reflections on Skating and Related Activities" (cover title: "The Only One-Legged Figure Skater, Ever"), unpublished typescript, University of Toronto Skating Club, p. 5.
7. Ibid.
8. Ibid., 6.
9. Ibid., 8-9.
10. Falkner received the medical care he needed under provisions of the Soldiers' Civil Re-establishment Act, including fitting for a prosthesis. About fourteen thousand amputation and orthopaedic cases had received attention between Apr. 1, 1918, and Jan. 3, 1920. *Canada Year Book*, 1919 (Ottawa: King's Printer for the Dominion Bureau of Statistics, 1920), 671.
11. Falkner mentions the rink by name; its existence is corroborated in a 1918 advertisement, "Skating at the Greenaway Rink," Saskatoon *Daily Star*, Feb. 21, 1918.
12. After World War 1 returned soldiers could get farm land under the Soldier Settlement Act of 1919, but clearly farming was not an option for amputees. Although there was no guarantee of jobs for the war disabled, the federal government did provide vocational training. By December 31, 1919, 42,679 courses had been granted with pay and allowances. *Canada Year Book* 1919, 671-72. Measures such as the present Cosmopolitan Industries sheltered workshops, providing jobs for handicapped people, were not launched in Saskatoon until the 1960s.
13. John Booker, "Tribute to Norman A. Faulkner [sic]: 1893-1985," n.p., n.d., copy available in the Saskatoon Public Library Local History Room.
14. *Heroes, Rogues, Adventurers, and Trailblazers* produced by CinePost in association with the Saskatoon Public Library Local History Room for SCN, 2000, based on a photographic exhibition entitled "Rogues, Heroes, Adventurers and Trailblazers," curated by the author in 1999.

NOTES TO MORRIS COHEN

1. Daniel Levy, *Two-Gun Cohen: a Biography* (New York: St. Martin's Press, 1997). Levy has been a reporter for *Time* and currently works for *People* magazine.
2. In his 1916 attestation papers Cohen claimed he was born in London, but biographer Daniel Levy indicates he was born in Poland before his father immigrated to England.
3. Daniel Levy, text panel for "Rogues, Heroes, Adventurers and Trailblazers," photographic exhibition at Saskatoon Public Library, curated by the author, 1999.
4. Charles Drage, *Two-Gun Cohen* (London: Jonathan Cape, 1954).
5. Dr. Thomas Barnardo was founder of a philanthropic society that sent poor and orphaned British children abroad to work on farms or as domestics.
6. Cyril Edel Leonoff, *Wapella Farm Settlement (The First Successful Jewish Farm Settlement in Canada): A Pictorial History* (Historical & Scientific Society of Manitoba, and Jewish Historical Society of Western Canada, [1970]), 5.
7. Or Nickelson, as spelled in *Mingling Memories: A History of Wapella and Districts* (Wapella History Book Committee, 1979), 64.
8. In the Drage book, Cohen mistakenly recalls that he first went to Winnipeg, then Moose Jaw. Author Daniel Levy straightened this out by tracking down the date the Norris & Rowe circus came to Moose Jaw.
9. Peter S. Li, "Chinese Immigrants on the Canadian Prairie, 1910-1947," *Canadian Review of Sociology and Anthropology* 19, no. 4 (1982): 530.
10. "City Police Raid a Chinese Joint," Saskatoon *Phoenix*, Sept. 5, 1910.
11. "Alleged Pickpocket Put Under Arrest: Interesting Story Told by Ire Toder...," Saskatoon *Phoenix*, Sept. 7, 1910, p. 8; "Maurice [sic] Cohen Sent to Jail: Creates a Scene in Court When Sentence is Pronounced," Saskatoon *Phoenix*, Sept. 9, 1910, p. 8; "Pickpocket Charge Dark Against Cohen: But the Accused Denies the Whole Story...," Saskatoon *Phoenix*, Sept. 8, 1910.
12. It is ironic that the Chinese were arrested in a British colony for smoking opium when it was the British who introduced that particular scourge into China.
13. Cohen omitted this caper in his own "told-to" autobiography, but author Daniel Levy turned up this tidbit in Cohen's medical records.
14. Ray Crone, "The Unknown Air Force," *Saskatchewan History* 30, no. 1 (winter 1970).
15. Qing-ling is now spelled Qingling, and Mei-ling is Meiling.
16. Drage, *Two-Gun Cohen*, 288.
17. Ibid., 149.
18. Biographer Daniel Levy disputes most of these claims.
19. Kendall (sometimes spelled Kendal) was later involved in a spectacular group escape from Hong Kong just as the Japanese were storming the gates. See Oliver Lindsay, *At the Going Down of the Sun: Hong Kong and South-East Asia 1941-1945* (London: Hamish Hamilton, 1981), chap. 2.

20. This account has been backed up by other prisoners describing treatment of would-be escapers.
21. Saskatoon *StarPhoenix*, Sept. 7, 1945.
22. "Prepare Evacuation of Canadian P.O.W. from Hong Kong," Saskatoon *StarPhoenix*, Sept. 5, 1945. Saskatchewan POWs released included George Porteous (later lieutenant-governor of Saskatchewan), Regina Sergeant R. J. Routledge (Saskatoon *StarPhoenix*, Sept. 10, 1945, p. 3.), and Private Urban Vernette of Prince Albert (Saskatoon *StarPhoenix*, Sept. 9, 1945).
23. Dave McIntosh, *Hell on Earth: Aging Faster, Dying Younger: Canadian Prisoners of the Japanese During World War II* (Toronto: McGraw-Hill Ryerson Limited, 1997), 14 and 194 (citing diary of Sergeant Lance Ross, published in *The Royal Rifles of Canada in Hong Kong*).
24. Levy, *Two-Gun Cohen*, 234.
25. Drage, *Two-Gun Cohen*, 137.
26. *Jerusalem Post* website, http://www.jpost.com/Editions/200/04/19, page no longer exists, contact author for printout.
27. NBC website, http://members.nbci.com/_XMCM/1spy/cohenM.html, page no longer exists, contact author for printout.
28. Angelfire website, http://www.angelfire.com/dc/1spy/film/html, page no longer exists, contact author for printout.
29. *Morris "Two-Gun" Cohen,* video produced by Magic Lantern for Great North Productions Inc. in association with History Television and the CRB Foundation's Heritage Project, [199?].
30. "Gen. Morris Cohen, Bodyguard of Dr. Sun Yat-sen, Dies at 84," *New York Times,* Sept. 14, 1970, p. 39.
31. *Kirkus Reviews,* June 15, 1997.

Sources Not Cited in Endnotes

Chinatown on the Prairies: the Emergence of an Ethnic Community. Selected papers from the Society for the Study of Architecture in Canada, Annual Meeting 1975 and 1976. Ottawa: The Society, 1975-1983.

Clubb, O. Edmund. *20th Century China.* 3d ed. New York: Columbia University Press, 1978.

McIntosh, Dave. *Hell on Earth: Aging Faster, Dying Younger: Canadian Prisoners of the Japanese During World War II.* Toronto: McGraw-Hill Ryerson Limited, 1997.

NOTES TO JEAN EWEN

1. Bruce Ewen, Regina, telephone interview and correspondence, Nov. 1998.
2. Laura Meyer, interview in Victoria, Feb. 11, 2003.
3. Harry Ewen (Jean's nephew), interviews and correspondence, 1998-2002.

4. He worked as a blacksmith for Harold Fletcher in 1923, and thereafter for Riddel Motor and Carriage Works, but annual city directories report a householder's employment only on a given day of the year, so a business of his own could have escaped the survey.
5. Tom's contributions to the labour movement were noted by labour historian Glen Makahonuk in "'Twixt Hammer and Anvil: the Saskatoon Smithy Workers' Strike," *Saskatchewan History* 42, no. 2 (spring 1989): 49-61.
6. Gregory S. Kealey and Reg Whitaker, eds., *R.C.M.P. Security Bulletins: the War Series, 1939-41* (St. John's: Committee on Canadian Labour History, 1989).
7. Laura Meyer, telephone interview, 1998.
8. Tom McEwen, *The Forge Glows Red: From Blacksmith to Revolutionary* (Toronto: Progress Books, 1974).
9. Political adversaries in China called each other bandits, white or red. In 1936 Edgar Snow was told that editors of newspapers "must call them bandits because they are ordered to do so by Nanking." Nanking was the seat of Chiang Kai-shek's government. Edgar Snow, *Red Star Over China* (New York: Grove Press, 1978; first published by Random House, 1938), 10.
10. Chinese place-names can be a nightmare to non-Chinese, with profuse spelling inconsistencies. These were compounded when the Latinized version of Chinese was changed from the old Wade system of phonetic transliteration to the Pin Yin alphabet. Thus Peking/Peiping became Beijing; Shensi and Shansi became Shanxi and Shaanxi; Sian/Hsian became Xian, and so forth.
11. "Weapons of Mass Destruction," *National Geographic* (Nov. 2002), 2-35.
12. Tom Kozar, telephone interview, Oct. 2003.
13. "440 Die as Shell Razes Shanghai Shopping Area," Saskatoon *StarPhoenix*, Aug. 23, 1937.
14. "Nurse in China," portrait with caption, Vancouver *Province*, Feb. 3, 1938.
15. From *China Nurse* by Jean Ewen. Used by permission. McClelland & Stewart Ltd., The Canadian Publishers.
16. Carlson mentions Ewen several times in *Twin Stars of China* (New York: Dodd, Mead & Company, 1940). He notes she "spoke Chinese with great facility" and corroborates accounts of enemy bombardment.
17. Tom Newnham, "Kathleen Hall, Dr. Bethune's Angel," first published in *China Today* and reproduced on www.nzchinasociety.org.nz/kathleenarticle.html, Aug. 22, 2002.
18. American journalist Edgar Snow wrote at some length in *Red Star Over China* (pp. 340-47) about the "little Red Devils" of the Young Vanguard who accompanied the Red Army. They served as nurses, couriers, and even spies.
19. Smedley was involved in movements pushing for birth control and independence for India. After her time in China she helped form a civil rights group that defended Hollywood victims of McCarthyism.
20. "Soldier Son Greets Tom Ewen, Released from Internment" (photo caption),

and accompanying article "Free Five More Communists to Fight 'Harder Than Ever,'" Toronto *Daily Star,* Oct. 13, 1942.
21. Conversation with Tom Kozar, Vancouver, Feb. 14, 2003.
22. Jean Ewen, *China Nurse* (Toronto: McClelland & Stewart, 1981), later issued in paperback as *Canadian Nurse in China.*
23. Canadian Broadcasting Corporation interviews with Jean Ewen aired on "This Morning" Aug. 31, 1976, and "As It Happens," Aug. 30, 1976.
24. "The Burial Ceremony of Jean Ewen's Ashes Held in Tanxian," *People's Daily,* May 24, 1988.

Sources Not Cited in Endnotes

Allan, Ted, and Sydney Gordon. *The Scalpel, the Sword.* Toronto: McClelland and Stewart, 1952.
Clubb, O. Edmund. *Twentieth Century China,* 3d ed. New York: Columbia University Press, 1978.
"The Fighting McEwens: Vote McEwen," election poster from Yukon *Progress,* personal collection of Tom Kozar, Vancouver.
Maxwell, Dorothy. "Journey to China with the Family of Jean Ewen Kovich to Transport Her Bone Ashes,"[ca. 1988]. Typescript, City of Victoria Archives.
Murphy, Patrick. "China Junket Honors Medical Heroes," Victoria *Times-Colonist,* Feb. 10, 1994.
"Nurse's Ashes Going to China," Victoria *Times-Colonist,* May 14, 1988.
Wilson, John. *Norman Bethune: A Life of Passionate Conviction.* Montreal: XYZ Publishers, 1999.
Stewart, Roderick. *The Mind of Norman Bethune.* Toronto: Fitzhenry & Whiteside, 1977 and 2002.

NOTES TO GLADYS ARNOLD

1. University of Regina Archives and Special Collections, Arnold Papers, Box 28, File 675.
2. Arnold Papers, Box 28, File 676.
3. Letter to Joe Chilco, Jan. 23, 1988, Arnold Papers, 98-54, Box 27, File 669.
4. Gladys Arnold, "At the Spanish Border," Winnipeg *Free Press,* Feb. 25, 1939, editorial page.
5. Karen Boyd, "Canadian Journalist Recalls German Occupation," *Arizona Republic,* Dec. 2, 1976.
6. Herbert R. Lottman, *The Fall of Paris June 1940* (New York: HarperCollins Publishers, 1940).
7. Letter to Joe Chilco, Jan. 23, 1988.
8. Letter to her mother, Paris, May 20 or 28 [illegible], 1940, Arnold Papers, 98-54, Box 5, File 27.

9. "Army Cooking Set-up Somebody's Headache," n.d., CP dispatch, Arnold Papers, 98-54, Box 28, File 676.
10. Boyd, "Canadian Journalist."
11. Lottman, *The Fall of Paris,* 290.
12. Richard Needham, 'They Were Too Young to Know Their Names," Calgary *Herald,* Jan. 17, 1941.
13. Lottman, *The Fall of Paris,* 266.
14. "Buy a Tank for France: Saskatoon Plans Blitzkreig Fund for Aid of Ally," Saskatoon *StarPhoenix,* June 12, 1940, p. 3. A postcard of this tank is housed in the Saskatoon Public Library Local History Room.
15. "Round-up of Italians," Saskatoon *StarPhoenix,* June 13, 1940, editorial page.
16. "Miss G. Arnold Caught in Flow of Humanity Streaming from Paris," Saskatoon *StarPhoenix,* datelined London, June 24, 1940 (CP), Arnold Papers, 98-54, Box 28, File 676.
17. Ibid.
18. Gladys Arnold, interview, Regina, Mar. 29, 2001.
19. Letter to her mother, June 25 or 28, 1940, Arnold Papers, 98-54, Box 5, File 27.
20. "Harrowing War Trip Made Her Sad, Angry," Ottawa *Journal,* Sept. 30, 1976.
21. "Journalist Recalls Tragic Experiences in War-Torn France...," Victoria *Daily Times,* [Feb. 8?] 1941.
22. Canadian Press dispatch, Aug. 16 [1940], Arnold Papers, 98-54, Box 28, File 675.
23. Carolyn Cox and Rica Farquaharson, "Women in Free France" (n.p., n.d.), Arnold Papers, 98-54, Box 28, File 683.
24. "Three Free French Movement Women Tell of Struggle," Kamloops *Sentinel,* June 13, 1945 or 1946, Arnold Papers, 98-54, clippings file 683.
25. Gladys Arnold, *One Woman's War: a Canadian Reporter with the Free French* (Toronto: James Lorimer & Company, 1987), 216.
26. *The Making of a Secret Agent,* ed. by George H. Ford (Toronto: McClelland and Stewart, 1978).
27. Letter from Joe Chilco, Jan. 23, 1988.
28. Interview with Gladys Arnold and Barry Robins (cousin), Mar. 29, 2001.
29. "Canadian Woman Recognized by France's Highest Honor," Sudbury *Star,* Mar. 13, 1971; Alixe Carter, "France Honours Gladys Arnold," Ottawa *Journal,* Mar. 12, 1971.
30. Marjorie Gillies, "Writing Behind the Front Lines," Ottawa *Citizen,* May 11, 1987.
31. Letter from Joe Chilco, Jan. 23, 1988.
32. "1,000 Graduate from U of R," Regina *Leader-Post,* May 21, 1988.
33. "One Woman's War Reporter: Grace [sic] Arnold 1905-2002," Toronto *Globe and Mail,* Oct. 11, 2002.
34. *Eyewitness to War,* Dir. Barbara Campbell and Daryl K. Davis, videocassette, Cooper Rock Pictures Inc., 2001.

Sources Not Cited in Endnotes

Davidson, Edward and Dale Manning. *Chronology of World War II*. London: Cassell & Co., 1999.
Keegan, John. *The Second World War*. New York: Penguin Books, 1989.
May, Ernest R. *Strange Victory: Hitler's Conquest of France*. New York: Hill and Wang, 2000.
Robbins, Barry. Interview. Regina, Mar. 29, 2001.

NOTES TO FATHER JOHN CLAFFEY

1. J. P. Gallagher, *Scarlet Pimpernel of the Vatican* (London: Souvenir Press, 1967).
2. *The Scarlet and the Black,* motion picture and videocassette, ITC Productions Inc., 1983.
3. John Cornwall, *Hitler's Pope: The Secret History of Pius XII* (New York: Penguin Books, 1999).
4. Dr. Salim Diamand, *Dottore! Internment in Italy 1940-45* (Oakville, New York, London: Mosaic Press, 1987), 63, 67.
5. Dr. Daniel McFadden, unpublished eulogy, Nov. 1997, Saskatoon Catholic Centre.
6. Maria de Blasio Wilhelm, *The Other Italy: the Italian Resistance in World War II* (New York, London: W.W. Norton & Company, 1988).
7. Gallagher, *Scarlet Pimpernel of the Vatican,* 175.
8. John Windsor, *The Mouth of the Wolf* (Sidney, B.C.: Gray's Publishing Ltd., 1967).
9. Father Ron Beechinor, telephone interview, Nov. 29, 2002.
10. Obituary, Saskatoon *StarPhoenix,* Nov. 22, 1997.
11. Art Robinson, "Unsung Hero: Priest Reluctant to Grave About Valiant War Service," Saskatoon *StarPhoenix,* Nov. 1984; copy from Saskatoon Catholic Centre.

Sources Not Cited in Endnotes

Heaps, Leo. *The Evaders*. New York: Morrow Publishing, 1976.
Keagan, John. *The Second World War*. New York: Penguin Books, 1989. First published by Century Hutchinson in 1989.
Trevelyan, Raleigh. *Rome '44: the Battle for the Eternal City*. New York: Viking Press, 1981.
Weymouth, Guy. *A.W.O.L.: in an Italian Prison Camp and Subsequent Adventures on the Run in Italy 1943-1944*. London: Tom Donovan, 1993.
Zucotti, Susan. *The Italians and the Holocaust: Persecution, Rescue, Survival*. New York: Basic Books Inc, 1987.

NOTES TO JOAN FLETCHER

1. "She Gave Orders – the Japs Obeyed!" Regina *Leader-Post*, Oct. 30, 1946, p. 6.
2. The Dept. of External Affairs exempted her from regulations prohibiting women and children from travelling to war zones. She was allowed to embark between Oct. 30, 1940 and Jan. 30, 1941. Letter from Dept. of External Affairs, Oct. 3, 1940.
3. *Soldier: the British Army Magazine* 1 no. 26 (Feb. 16, 1946): 12.
4. Beryl E. Escott, *Twentieth-Century Women of Courage* (London: Sutton Publishing, 1999) 60; FANY website:www.64bakerstreet/organizations/orgs_the_fany.html>.
5. The movie *Paradise Road* and the book *Songs of Survival* reflect the experiences of women and children in Japanese prison camps on Sumatra.
6. Canadian women volunteers packed 16,288,000 packages containing six million "articles of comfort." "Canadian Red Cross Spent $100,000,000 in War Years," Saskatoon *StarPhoenix*, Mar. 7, 1946, p. 3.
7. "Joan Fletcher Describes Singapore Red Cross Duties," Regina *Leader-Post*, Nov. 17, 1945.
8. John Terraine, *The Life and Times of Lord Mountbatten* (New York: Holt, Rinehart and Winston, 1968, 1980), 139.
9. Helen Colijn, *Song of Survival: Women Interned* (Ashland, Oregon: White Cloud Press, 1995), 208.
10. Capt. D. H. Clark, "Report over het werk van de RAPWI-groep in Bangkinang, 10 September 1945-11 November 1945," 1. Contact the author for a partial copy of this document.
11. Special Operations "Force 316," sent to blow up the newly-built bridge on the River Kwai, depicted in the film of the same name, may have been modelled on the real-life Force 136, although in truth the bridge was not blown up at that time.
12. "Nurse Home with Plastic Jaw, MBE," Vancouver *Sun*, Nov. 2, 1946, p. 2; and other articles.
13. "Japs Admire Canadian Woman Leader; But Think Her 'Too Tough' For Wife," Vancouver *Daily Province*, Oct. 29, 1946; and other articles.
14. "Plastic Jaw Souvenir of B.C. Girl's Heroism," Toronto *Star*, datelined Vancouver, Nov. 2, [1946].
15. *Soldier* magazine.
16. "Jap Gave Girl His Sword," *Daily Dispatch*, n.d., from Mabel Tibbenham's scrapbook of her sister's exploits, in possession of Barbara Campbell, Regina. After the war, Lt. Matsuo claimed this gift came from him. Fletcher had admired Captain Tachibana's ceremonial sword. He, Matsuo, gave his own sword to Captain Tachibana, and asked him to give his to Fletcher. Hollywood later used a version of the Samurai sword story in the 1988 film *Women*

of Valor starring Susan Sarandon, about American military nurses interned in a Japanese camp in the Philippines.
17. *Saturday Night,* Jan. 2 [1951?]; *Time,* Nov. 11, 1946; Manchester *Guardian,* Oct. 30, 1946; [London?] *Daily Mail,* [1946]. From Tibbenham scrapbook.
18. Larry Allen, "Polish Secret Police Fight 'Fifth Column'," Saskatoon *StarPhoenix,* Mar. 4, 1966.
19. "R.A.F. Saves Woman from Arrest." *Express,* n.p., n.d. (ca. Oct. 30, 1950). From Tibbenham scrapbook.
20. Letter from Arthur N. Miyazawa, Tokyo, to Madge Tibbenham, Sept. 12, 1979; copy in the Canadian War Museum.
21. "In the Honor of Miss. Lt. Fletcher," handwritten by former Lt. Daisaburo Matsuo, n.d., Canadian War Museum.
22. *Rescue from Sumatra,* dir. Barbara Campbell and Daryl K. Davis, videocassette, Cooper Rock Pictures Inc., 2001.

Sources Not Cited in Endnotes

Bharadwaj, Ramdev. *Sukarno and Indonesian Nationalism.* Delhi: Rahul Publishing House, 1997.
Friend, Theodore. *The Blue-Eyed Enemy: Japan Against the West in Java and Luzon, 1942-1945.* Princeton: Princeton University Press, 1988. Joan Bamford Fletcher collection, Canadian War Museum.
First Aid Nursing Yeomanry website: www.fany.org.uk.
Keegan, John. *The Second World War.* New York: Penguin Books, 1989.
Vlekke, Bernard H. M. *The Story of the Dutch East Indies.* Cambridge, Mass.: Harvard University Press, 1946.
Von Albertini, Rudolf. "The Decolonization of the Dutch East Indies." In *The End of European Empire: Decolonization After World War II,* edited by Tony Smith, 171-77. Toronto: D.C. Heath and Company, 1975.
See also the chapter on Morris "Two-Gun" Cohen in this book for further reading on prisoners of war in Japanese prison camps.

NOTES TO EMMA WOIKIN

1. Her birth was actually registered as January 1, 1921.
2. Woikin's nephew Fred Konkin played in those caves. Interview with Fred Konkin, Aug. 4, 2003, at Blaine Lake.
3. Ibid.
4. Ibid.
5. Photo and caption, Saskatoon *StarPhoenix,* Mar. 6, 1946, p. 1.
6. June Callwood, *Emma: the True Story of Canada's Unlikely Spy* (Toronto: Stoddart Publishing, 1984), 110.
7. *The Gouzenko Transcripts,* ed. Robert Bothwell and J. L. Granastein (Ottawa:

Deneau Publishers & Company Ltd., [1982?]), introduction.
8. Igor Gouzenko, *This Was My Choice* (J.M. Dent & Sons (Canada) Ltd., 1948).
9. William Stevenson, *A Man Called Intrepid: the Secret War* (New York and London: Harcourt Brace Jovanovich, 1976).
10. *The Most Dangerous Spy,* On Guard for Thee, a series on the Royal Canadian Mounted Police (National Film Board of Canada, 1981).
11. Prof. Benjamin DeForest Bayly, quoted in Bill Stevenson, *The True Intrepid: Sir William Stephenson* (Surrey, B.C.: Timberholme Books Ltd., 1998), 344-45. But David Stafford, author of Camp x, insists that Intrepid never found time to visit Camp x.
12. Bothwell and Granatstein, *The Gouzenko Transcripts,* 10.
13. J. W. Pickersgill and D. F. Forster, *The Mackenzie King Record 1945-1946* (Toronto: University of Toronto Press, 1970), 147.
14. "Churchill Speech Rapped by Pravda as Inciting War," Saskatoon *StarPhoenix,* Mar. 11, 1946.
15. "Grants Bail to Accused in Spy Ring," Saskatoon *StarPhoenix,* Mar. 13, 1946.
16. "All Dressed up" (photo and caption), Saskatoon *StarPhoenix,* Mar., 1946.
17. Pickersgill and Forster, *The Mackenzie King Record,* 14.
18. Canada, House of Commons *Debates,* 2nd session, 20th parliament, vol. 1, 1946, p. 140. The Star Chamber was an infamous court dating back to fifteenth-century England, named after stars painted on the ceiling of the king's special court where defendants were tried without access to rights guaranteed under British common law.
19. Mackenzie King diary entry dated Feb. 19, 1946, cited in Pickersgill and Forster, *The Mackenzie King Record,* 14.
20. Pickersgill and Forster, *The Mackenzie King Record,* 14.
21. Ian Fleming is said to have based the character to whom Bond reported on Intrepid (Stephenson). Fleming was involved in the British espionage world himself at the time.
22. "Spy Cells Existence is Denied," Saskatoon *StarPhoenix,* Mar. 12, 1946.
23. "French Impose Death Sentence Upon Spies," Saskatoon *StarPhoenix,* June 8, 1940, p. 1
24. "Asks Death for Spies," Saskatoon *StarPhoenix,* June 12, 1940.
25. Joseph Albright and Marcia Kunstel, *Bombshell: The Secret Story of Ted Hall and America's Unknown Atomic Spy* (New York: Times Books, 1997); *The Wall Street Journal,* Oct. 20, 1997; "Secrets, Lies and Atomic Spies," first broadcast on "Nova," PBS, Feb. 5, 2002.
26. "New Evidence in Spy Enquiry Too Important for Release," Saskatoon *StarPhoenix,* Dec. 7, 1948.
27. "Married Recently," Saskatoon *StarPhoenix,* n.d. [May, 1949?], Saskatoon Public Library Local History Room.
28. Konkin Interview, Aug. 4, 2003.
29. *The Most Dangerous Spy.*

30. John Diefenbaker, Canada, House of Commons *Debates*, 2nd session, 20th parliament, vol. 1, Mar. 15, 1946, p. 4.

Sources Not Cited in Endnotes

Hannant, Lawrence. "Igor Gouzenko and Canada's Cold War." *The Beaver* (October-November 1995): 19-23.
Hyde, H. Montgomery. *The Quiet Canadian: the Secret Service Story of Sir William Stephenson*. London: Constable & Company Limited, 1989, first published in 1962.
Sawatsky, John. *Gouzenko: the Untold Story*. Toronto: Macmillan of Canada, 1984.
Stafford, David. *Camp X: Canada's School for Secret Agents, 1941-45*. Toronto: Lester & Orpen Dennys Publishing, 1986.
Series of articles on Gouzenko case published in *StarPhoenix* throughout March, 1946, including "Churchill Warns Against Russian Expansionist Ideas," Mar. 4, p. 1; and "Conduct Inquiry Into Un-American State Personnel," Mar. 19, p. 1.
"Spies: Red Circles." *Newsweek* (July 29, 1946): 42.

NOTES TO RICHARD ST. BARBE BAKER

1. Confusion reigns regarding his surname. Because his father and brother Scott also had St. Barbe in their names, it was assumed it was like a hyphenated name. However, his birth certificate uses the surname Baker, as did the British *Who's Who*.
2. "Elderly Forester Still Looking for That Bear," *Post* [datelined Vancouver, CP], May 2, 1980; University of Saskatchewan Archives Alumni Office file on Richard St. Barbe Baker, June 1982.
3. Victor Whitbread, telephone interview, Aug. 7, 2003.
4. University of Saskatchewan calendar, 1911-12.
5. Autobiography [typescript], University of Saskatchewan Archives, Richard St. Barbe Baker Papers, A. 1, autobiography, 3, 1971.
6. "A Forester's Message," reprinted from *The Ecological Magazine*, October-November 1979, in *Man of the Trees*, ed. by Hugh Locke (Saskatoon: Richard St. Barbe Baker Foundation, 1984).
7. Saskatchewan Archives Board, Homestead Records, file no. 2134848.
8. The 1963 edition of *Who's Who* says he lived in Canada from 1909 to 1913.
9. Richard St. Barbe Baker, *Caravan Story and Country Notebook* (Wolverton, Bucks., England: McCorquedale & Co. Ltd., 1969), 9.
10. Nigel Wood, curator, West End Local History Museum & Heritage Centre, email correspondence, Aug. 21, 2003.
11. Sidney Walton, "Personal Notes," unpublished typescript, June 1960, University of Saskatchewan Archives, Baker papers, Series A.

12. Richard St. Barbe Baker, *My Life, My Trees* (London: Lutterworth Press, 1970).
13. Richard St. Barbe Baker, *The Redwoods* (London: Lindsay Drummond Ltd., 1943, 1946), 5.
14. *Encyclopedia of the Desert*, http:lexixonen.com, website no longer active, contact author for printout.
15. "Little Known Facts About Great Humanitarians: Richard St. Barbe Baker," n.p., n.d., University of Saskatchewan Archives, Baker Papers, Series A.
16. *Encyclopedia of the Desert*.
17. Marriage certificate, University of Saskatchewan Archives, Baker papers, Series B,II.
18. Baker, *My Life, My Trees*, 146.
19. William Vogt, Review, *New York Herald Tribune Book Review*, Nov. 20, 1949, p. 22.
20. Richard St. Barbe Baker, *Land of the Tané* (London: Butterworth, 1956), cited by Glenn Gustafson in "Richard St. Barbe Baker: Man of the Trees," *Saskatoon History Review* 9 (1994): 31.
21. "A Forester's Message."
22. "Little Known Facts."
23. Sydney Walton, "Richard St. Barbe Baker, Founder of the Men of the Trees: Forestry in New Zealand," typescript, University of Saskatchewan Archives, Baker papers, Series A.II.
24. "Little Known Facts."

Sources Not Cited in Endnotes

Baker, Richard St. Barbe. *Sahara Conquest*. London: Butterworth Press, 1966.
Eyre, Wayne. "The Man of the Trees: Richard St. Barbe Baker." *Green and White*, fall 1984, 17-20.
Saskatoon Public Library Local History Room. Clipping files.

ACKNOWLEDGMENTS

Gratefully I acknowledge the advice, assistance, and support of all those who helped me with this project, especially my family and friends who listened patiently while I bubbled away about some new discovery or wailed at difficulties encountered.

ARCHIVES
British Columbia Archives; Jeff O'Brien at City of Saskatoon Archives; Glenbow Archives & Library, especially Jim Bowman; Archives of Manitoba & Hudson's Bay Archives, especially Jennifer Simons; University of Manitoba Archives, especially Shelley Sweeney; National Archives of Canada; Saskatchewan Archives Board, Regina and Saskatoon, especially D'Arcy Hande, Nadine Charabin, and Tim Novak; University of Regina Archives, especially Selina Coward and Elizabeth Seitz; Margaret Sanche, St. Thomas More Archives; University of Saskatchewan Archives, especially Tim Hutchinson, Cheryl Avery, and Patrick Hayes; Victoria City Archives; University of Toronto Archives; Bruce Ibsen, City of Edmonton Archives; Betsy Gudz, University of Toronto Skating Club Archives; Yukon Archives.

HISTORIANS, AUTHORS, RESEARCHERS, AND OTHER INDIVIDUALS
Dr. Georgina Taylor, specialist in prairie history, for loan of books, advice on sources, and general wise counsel; Dr. Richard Rempel, historian emeritus, McMaster University, for advice on World War II sources

and general wise counsel; author Daniel S. Levy of Time-Warner; and Frank Roy for editing help; researcher Victor Whitbread for details on "St. Barbe" and others; local historians Bill Delainey and John Duerkop for many clever tips; Michael Flensburg, who helped me find antiquarian books; Wenda McArthur and Edna Alford who encouraged me with the book; Dolores Reimer and Alan Safarik for telling me about Parmer, and Harvey Mawson for advising on the Parmer chapter; Barbara Campbell, Regina writer and researcher, who gave me access to the Fletcher scrapbook; Gregory Salmers and his team of Dutch translators in Estevan; Alan Jensen for showing me the vintage *Smoky* film; Lise Perrault, Will James fan; Stephen McNeill of County Offaly Historical Society; Bill Barry regarding ferry locations, Janet Libke for taking me to the Bethune Museum, and historian Dr. Bill Waiser for valuable information on Will James.

Families and Friends of Subjects

Fred and Doreen Konkin, Blaine Lake, relatives of Emma Woikin; Laura Meyer of Victoria, Tom Kozar of Vancouver, the late Bruce Ewen of Regina, Harry Ewen of Delia, Alberta, relatives of Jean Ewen; Barry Robins, Gladys Arnold's cousin in Regina; Les and Louise Munson of Kelowna, related to the Hourie family; Bernadette McLoughlin, Stephen McNeill of Ireland, and Dr. McFadden of Saskatoon, for help with the Claffey story; Dr. Sidney Soanes and John Booker for information and referral on Norman Falkner; Pierre Dufault of Montreal and Robert Dufault of Ottawa, nephews of Will James; Gerald Clark, Mrs. Victor Cooper, and Josef Rich, relatives of Morris Cohen.

Libraries and Librarians

Saskatoon Public Library Local History Room staff, all the Information Services staff, Shelley Den Brok for telling me about Emma Woikin, and Jane Zhang for helping me with Chinese place names; Moose Jaw Public Library Local History Room; Nanaimo Public Library staff, especially Inge Vallat; Regina Public Library, especially Ken Aiken; librarian Bob Ivanochko, Saskatchewan Provincial Library, for significant biographical material sent; Toronto Reference Library staff; University of

Saskatchewan Library Special Collections and Government Documents staff, especially Andrew Hubbertz for guiding me through his collections; and Cambridge University staff for help with Baker's student record.

Media
Western Producer staff; the people at Saskatchewan Communications Network (SCN) and Cinepost Productions for helping to publicize some of the original biographies through the co-production of a series of short documentaries; Gail Donald and Lynda Barnett of CBC Archives.

Museums
Bethune Memorial House, Gravenhurst, Ontario; the Canadian War Museum; Dawson City Museum; Wilson Museum, Dundurn; Medicine Hat Museum; Snow Lake Museum, Manitoba; Sam Waller Museum, The Pas, Manitoba; Prince Albert Historical Museum; St. Marys Museum, Ontario, especially Mary Smith, curator; Irma Penn of the Jewish Heritage Centre of Western Canada.

Organizations
Harris Historical Society; Saskatoon Heritage Society; University of Toronto Figure Skating Club; Saskatoon Catholic Centre.

Others
Dr. Erasmus, who gave me back my precious sight, and all the myriad acquaintances and complete strangers who pointed me in new directions. Thanks also to editor Roberta Coulter and the staff of Coteau Books, and all those peer reviewers who provided valuable advice and information. Lastly I apologize to all those helpful people I have inadvertently neglected to mention – you know who you are.

Finally, the trouble with historical investigation is that it never ends. There's always a batch of fresh new sources popping up with contradictory information. At some point one's friends and colleagues begin to say, "publish already." It's time to wrap it up. And so, this is what I know so far.

PHOTO: JILLIAN MILLAR DRYSDALE

ABOUT THE AUTHOR

Ruth Wright Millar is a well-known Saskatoon historian, librarian and former journalist. She worked for many years in the local history room of the Saskatoon Public Library. She has made numerous appearances in publications such as the *Saskatoon StarPhoenix, Western People, Saskatoon History Review* and *Saskatchewan History*, and on radio and television programs, including "Basic Black." She has also published a number of short stories, written historical video scripts, and prepared historical photo exhibits and bibliographies.